Caryńskie Valley

Landscape and Nature Photo Book

Series: In the Bieszczady Mountains

Photos by
Jacek Lidwin

Table of contents:

Text about Caryńskie Valley 7

Beginning of photos 8

About author 49

The Caryńskie Valley is located in the Bieszczady Mountains in Poland. There in housed a village. Its inhabitants were forcibly displaced in 1946 to the USSR. Currently, only a few people live in it.

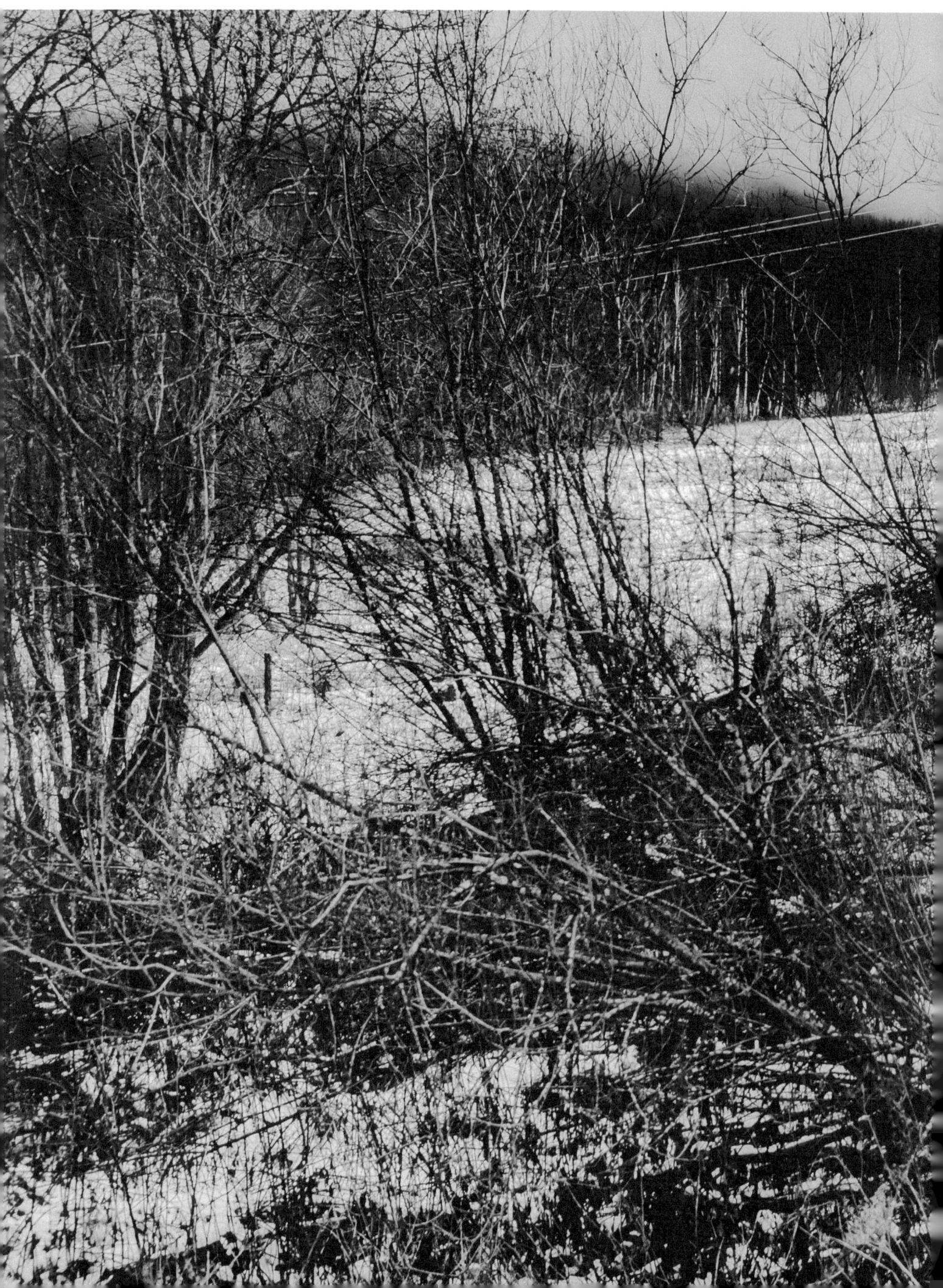

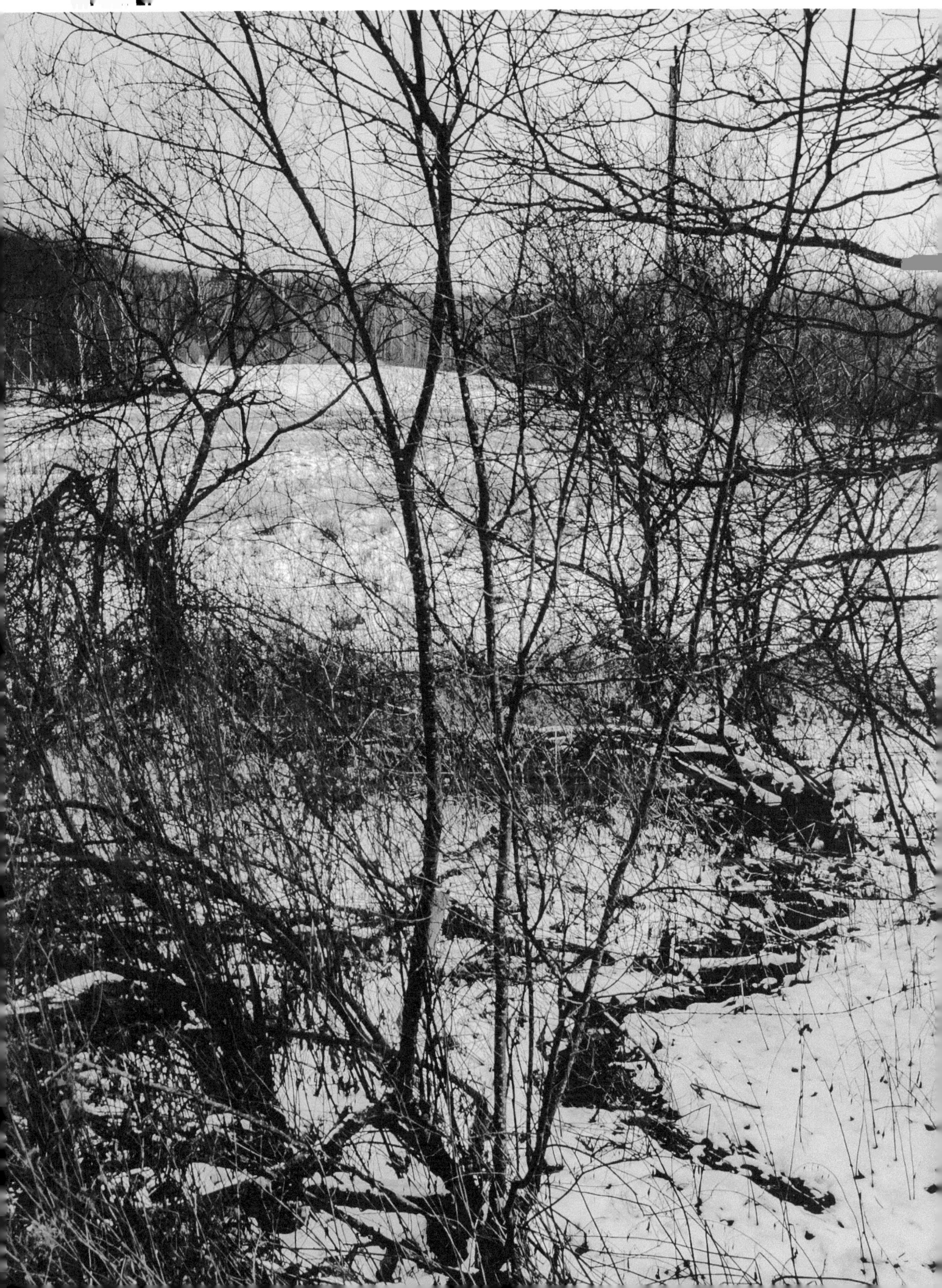

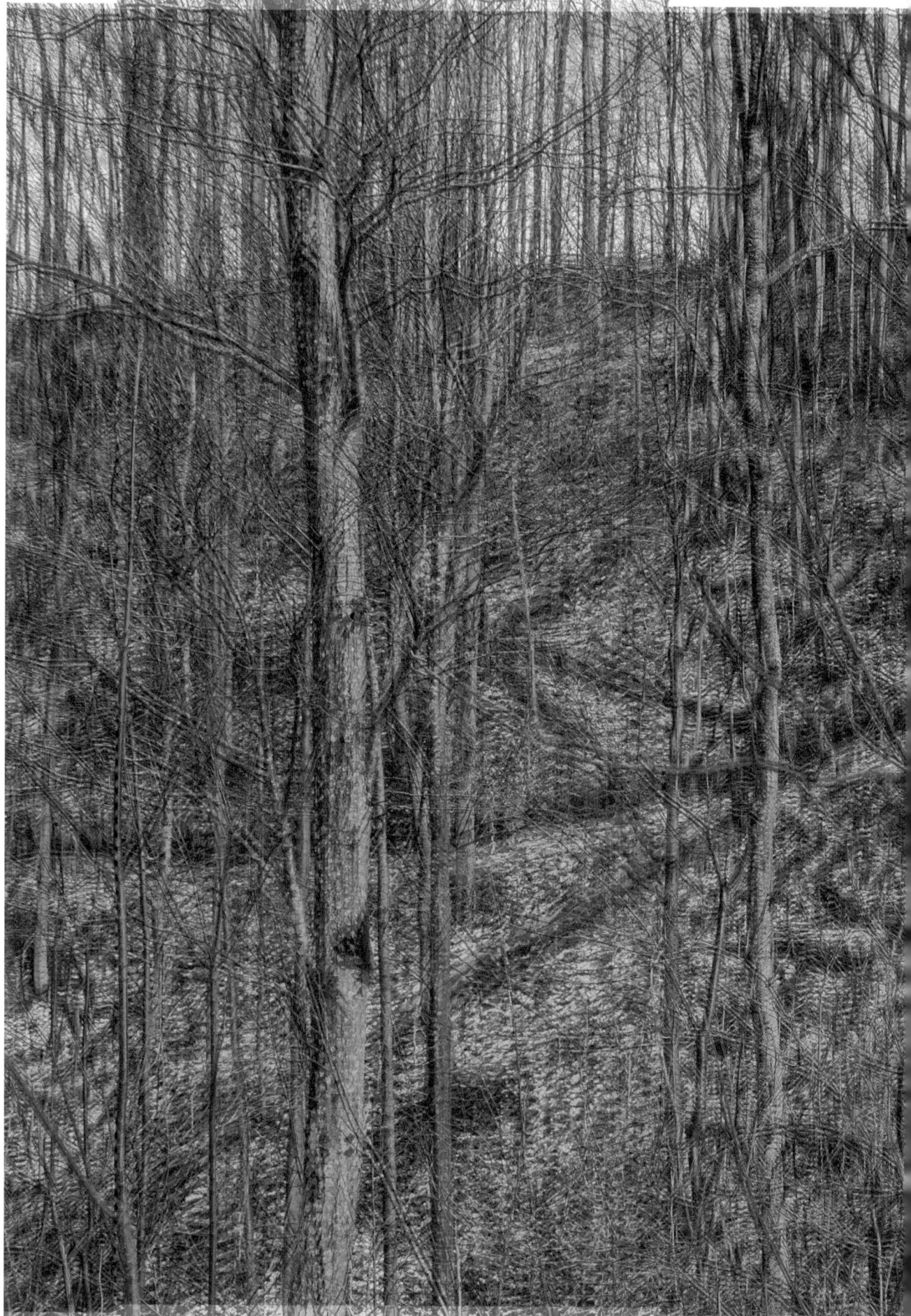

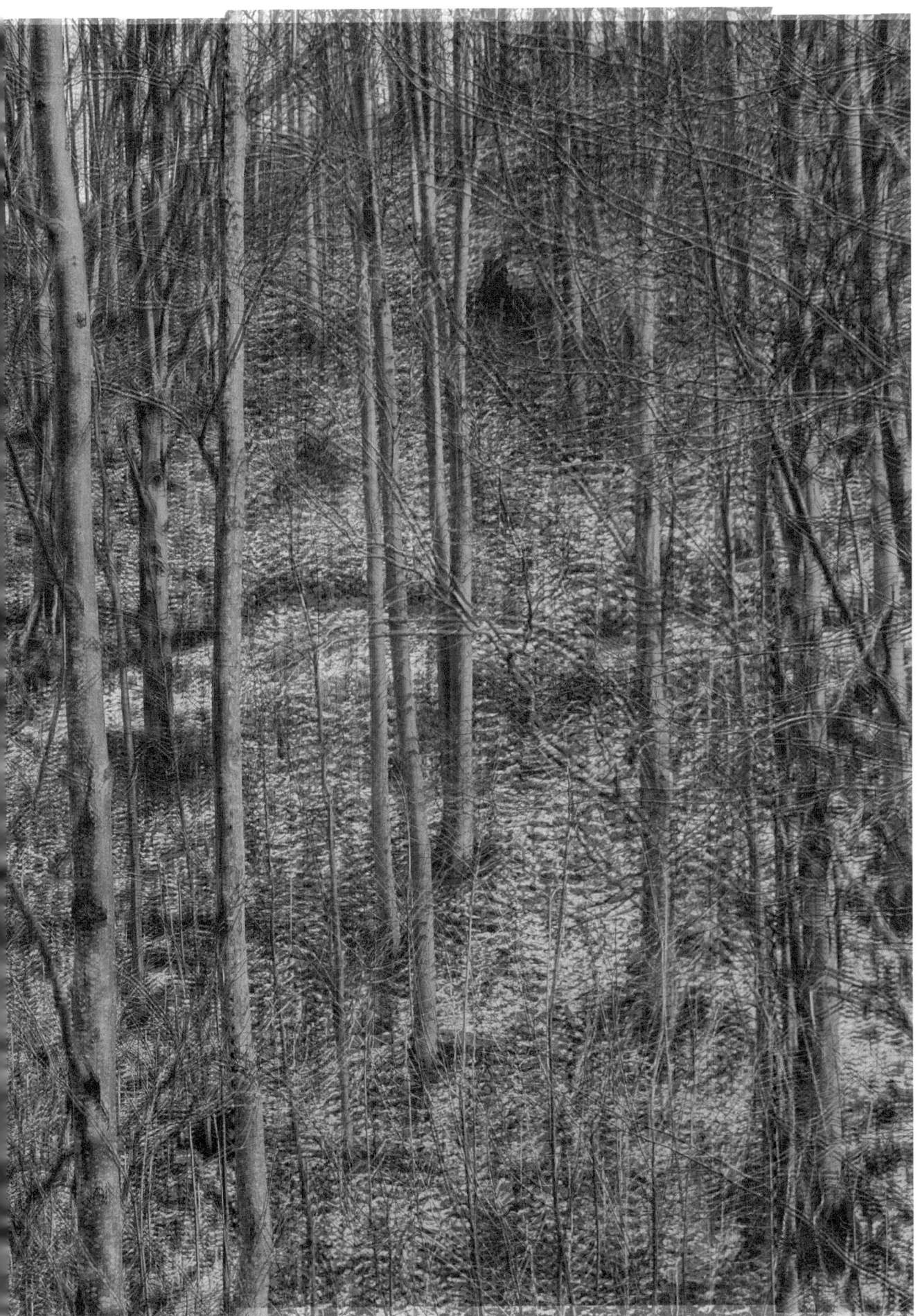

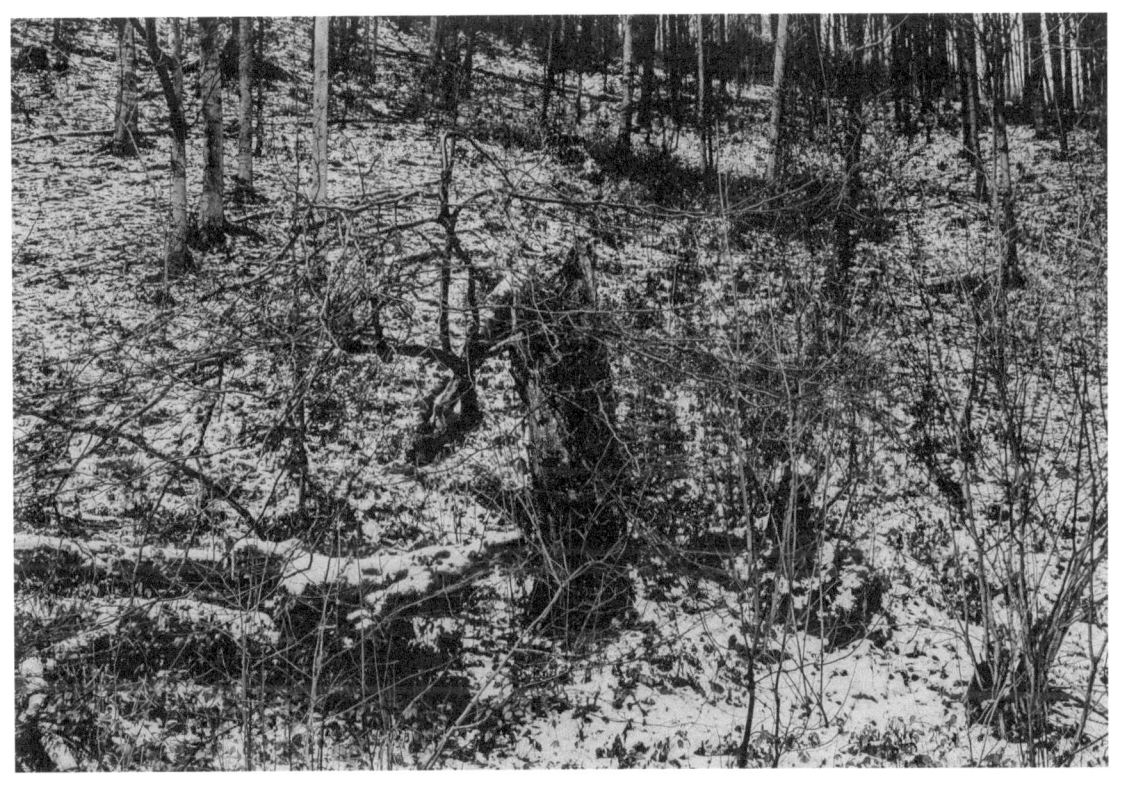

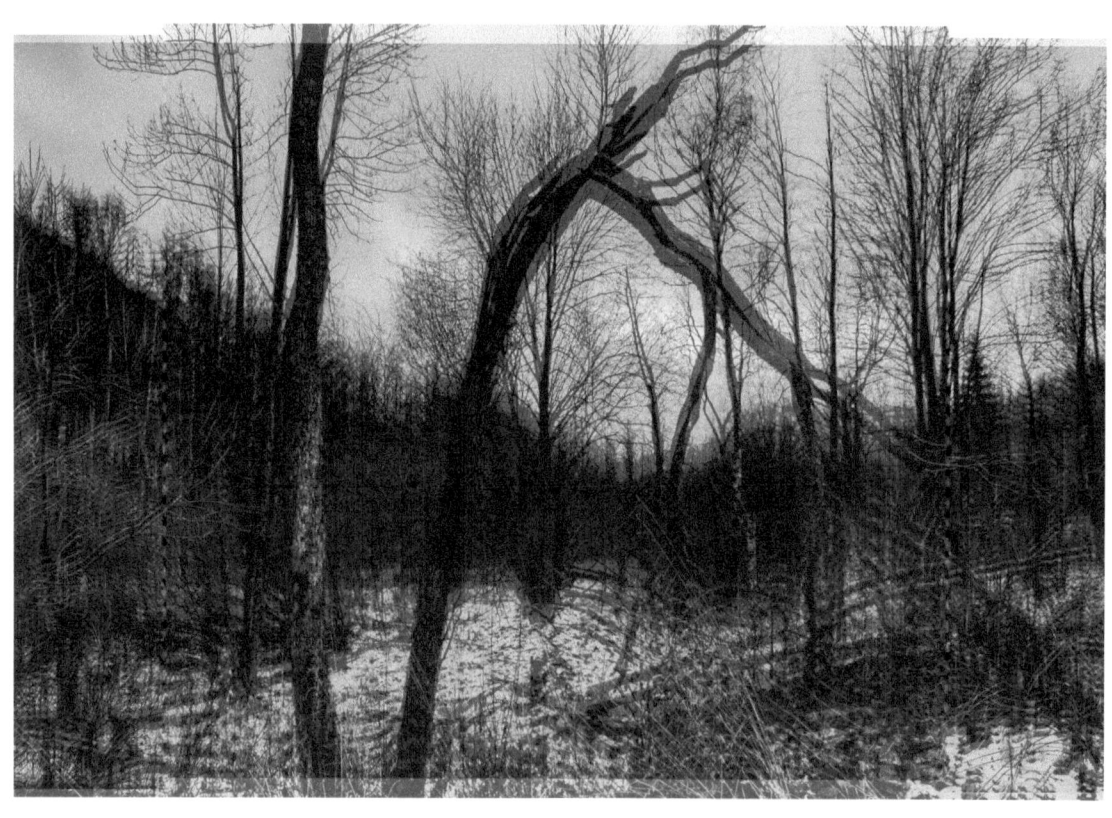

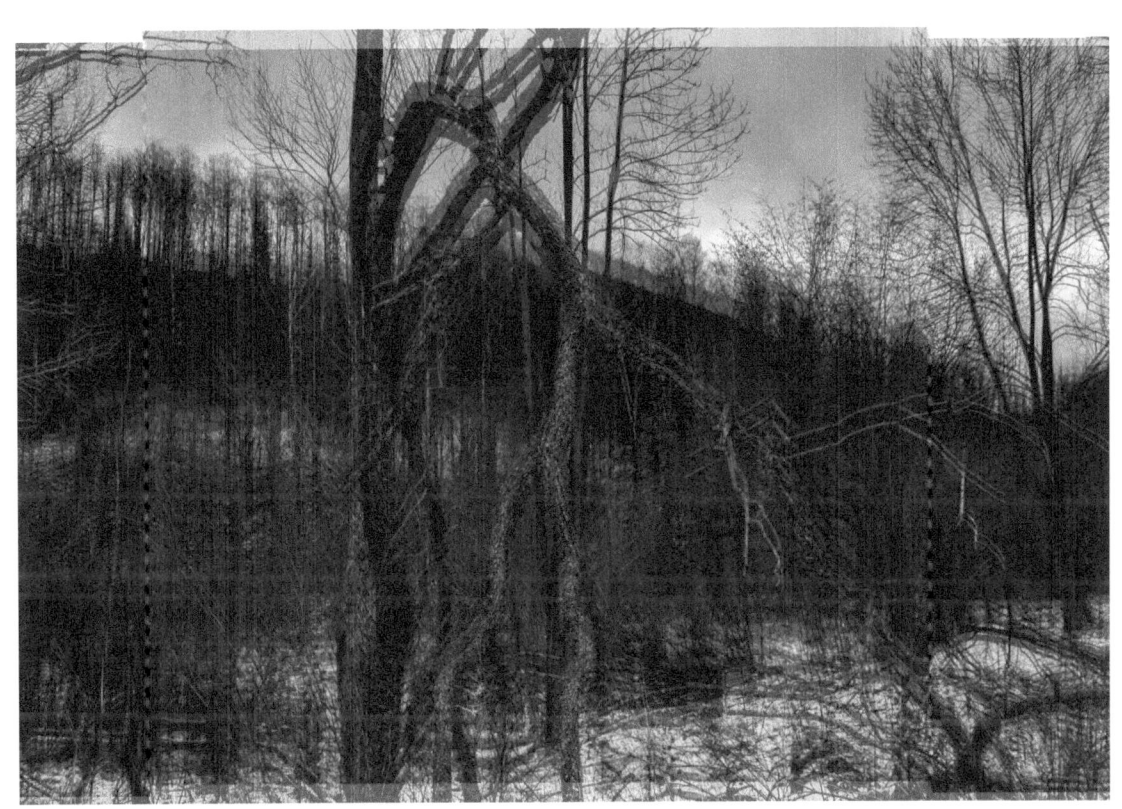

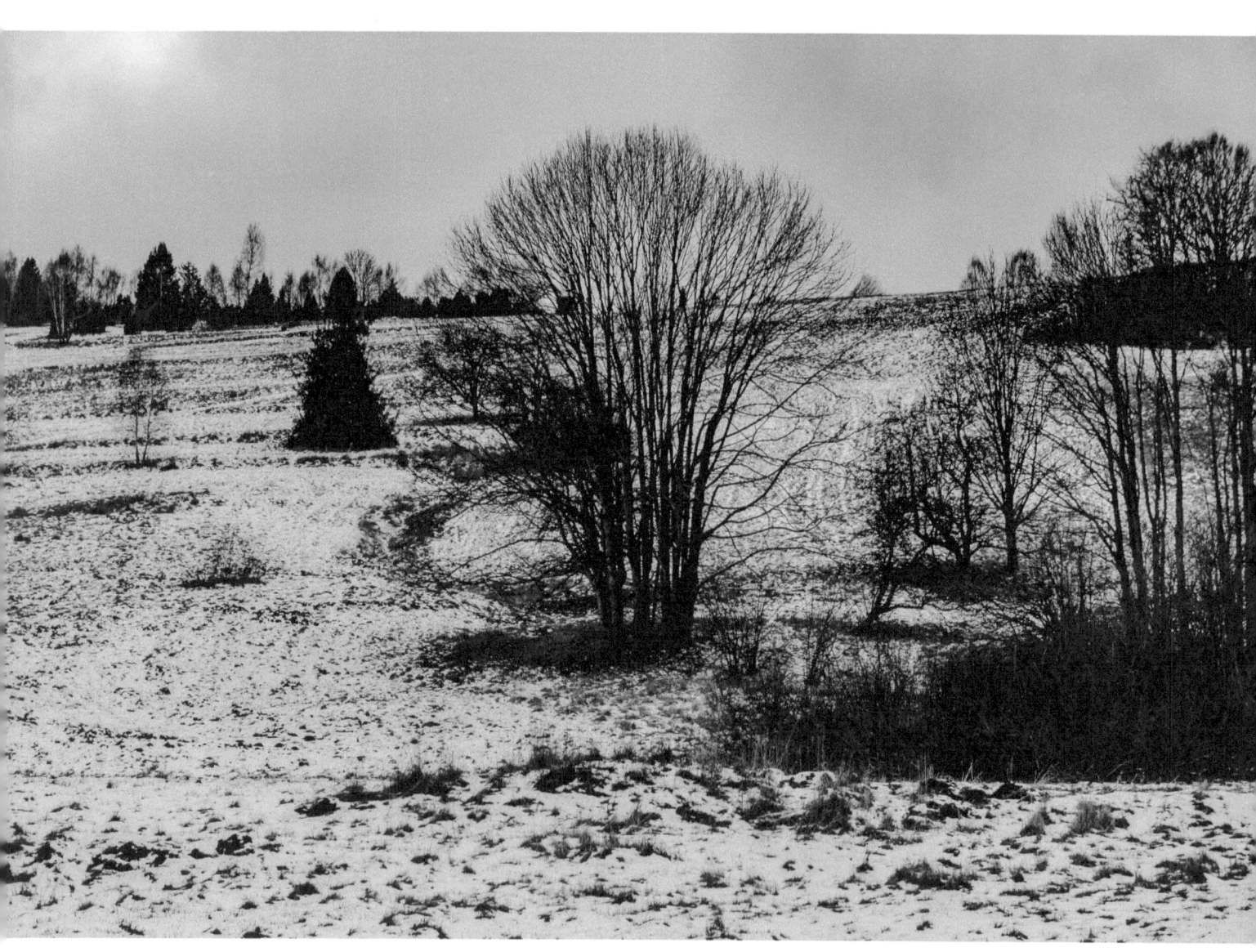

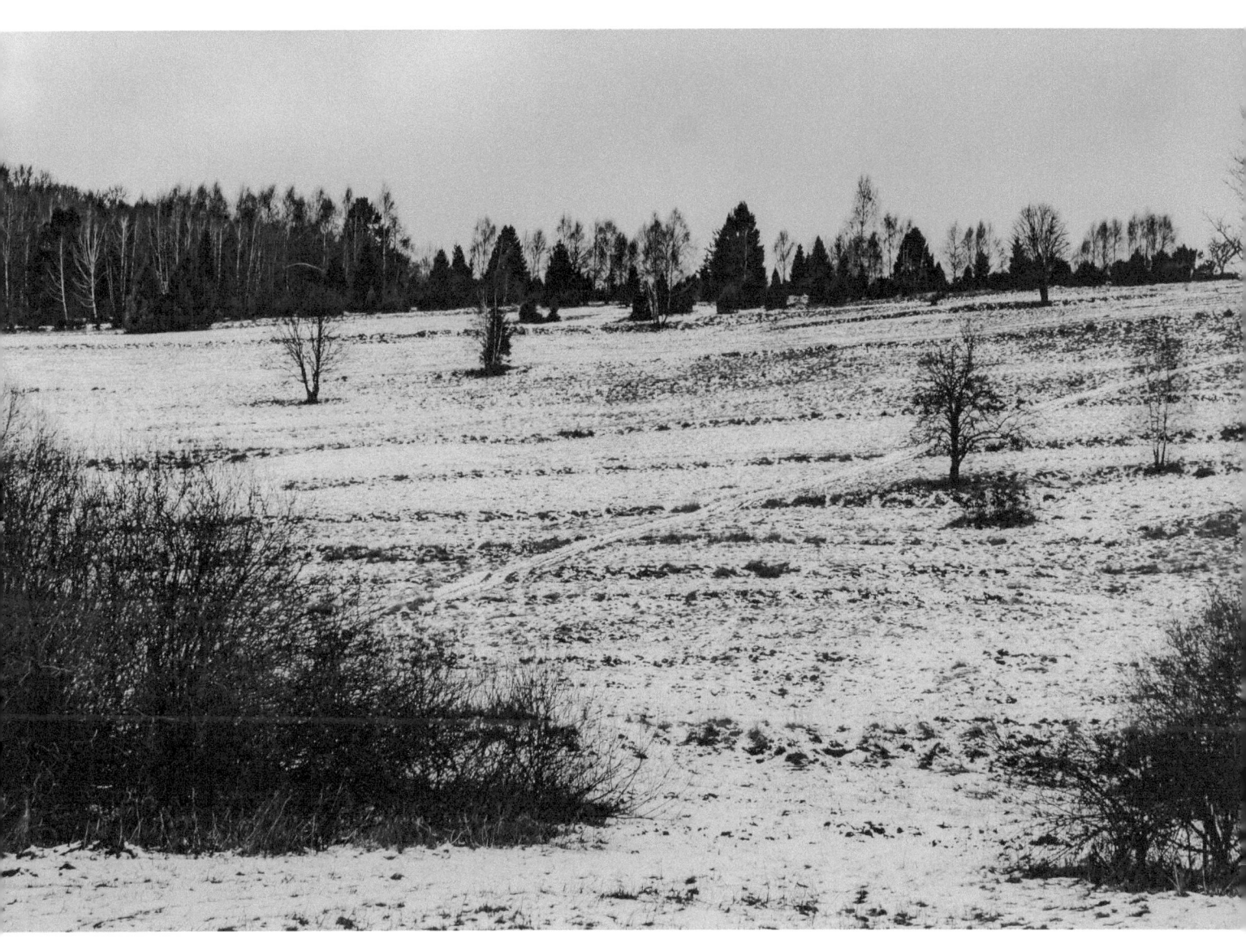

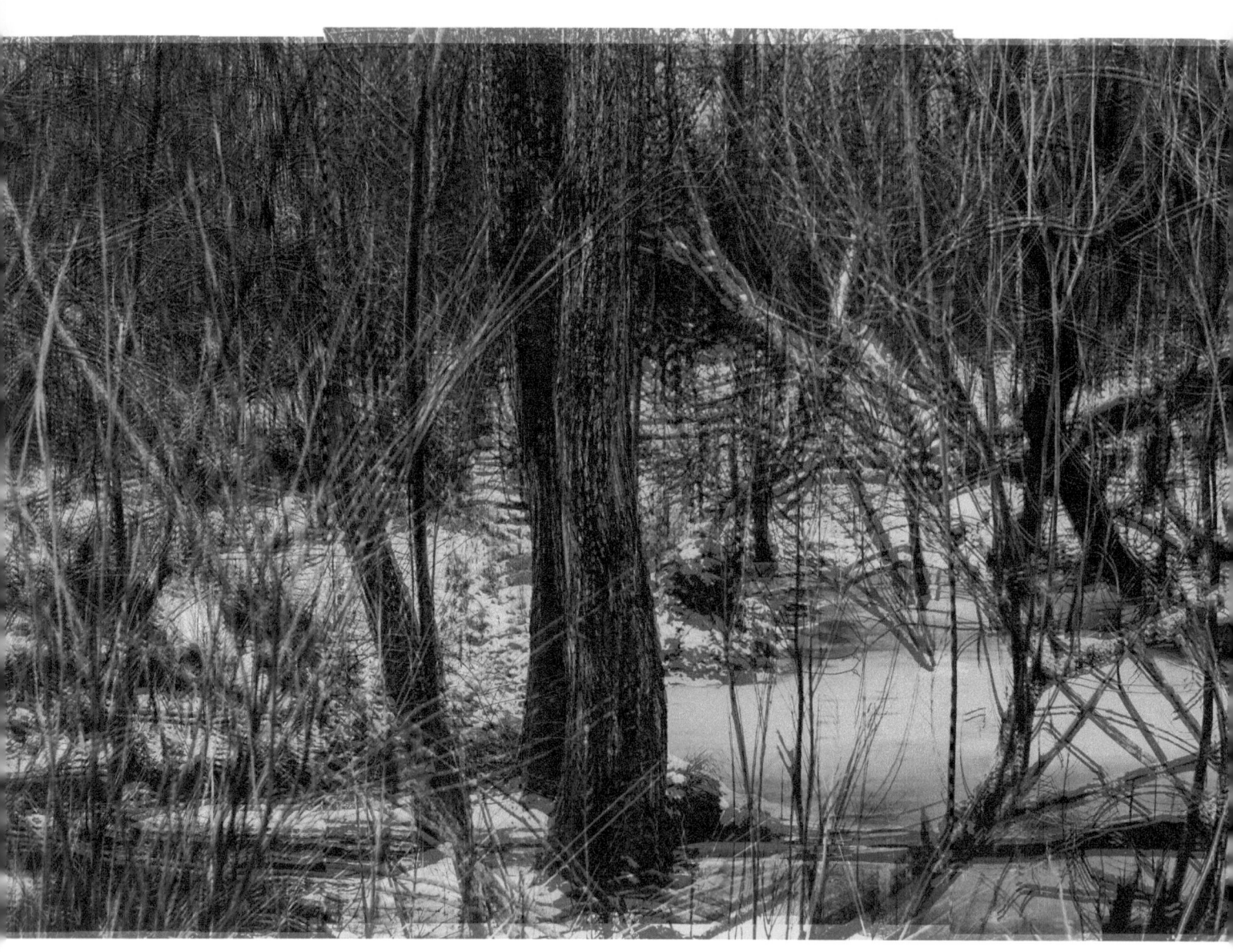

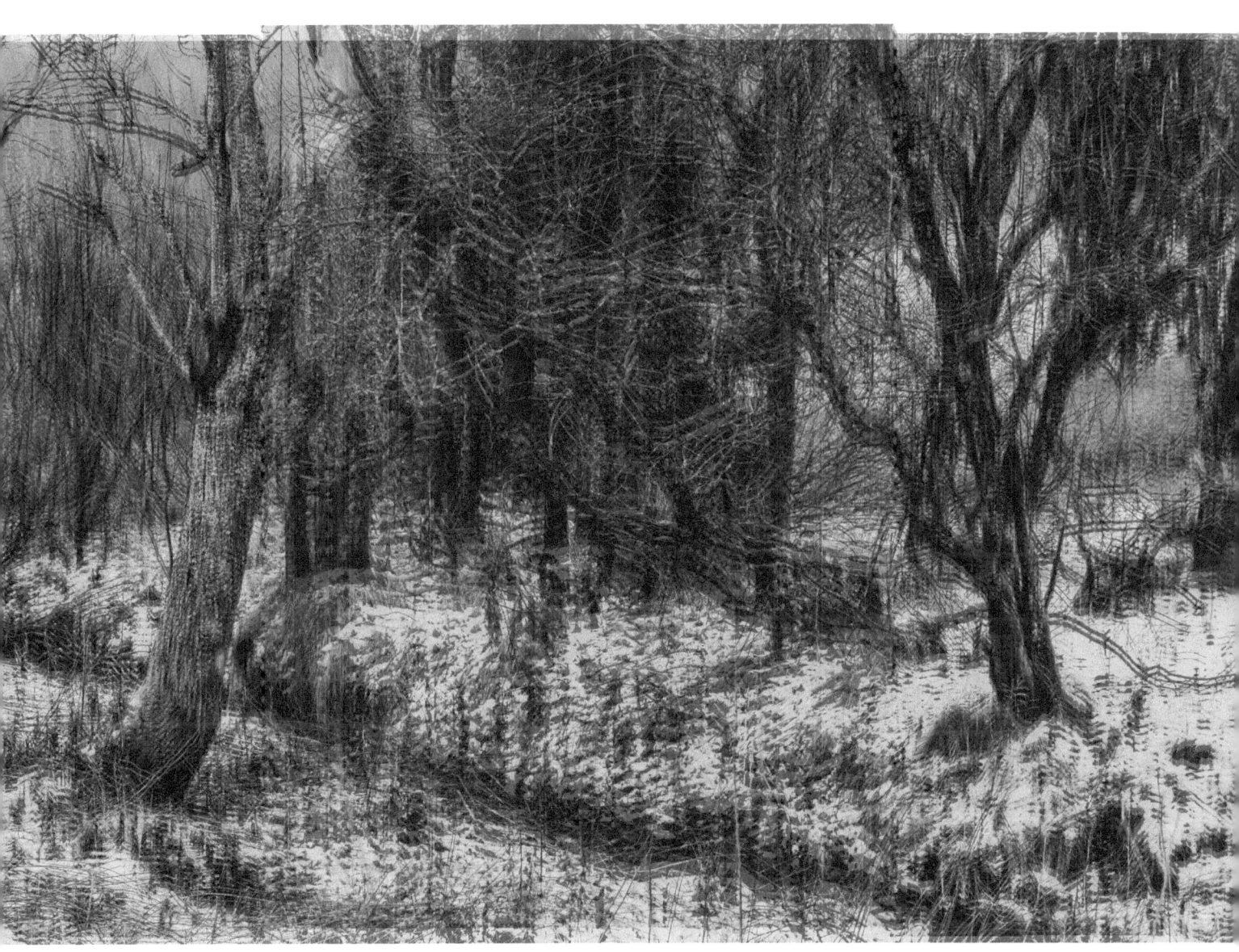

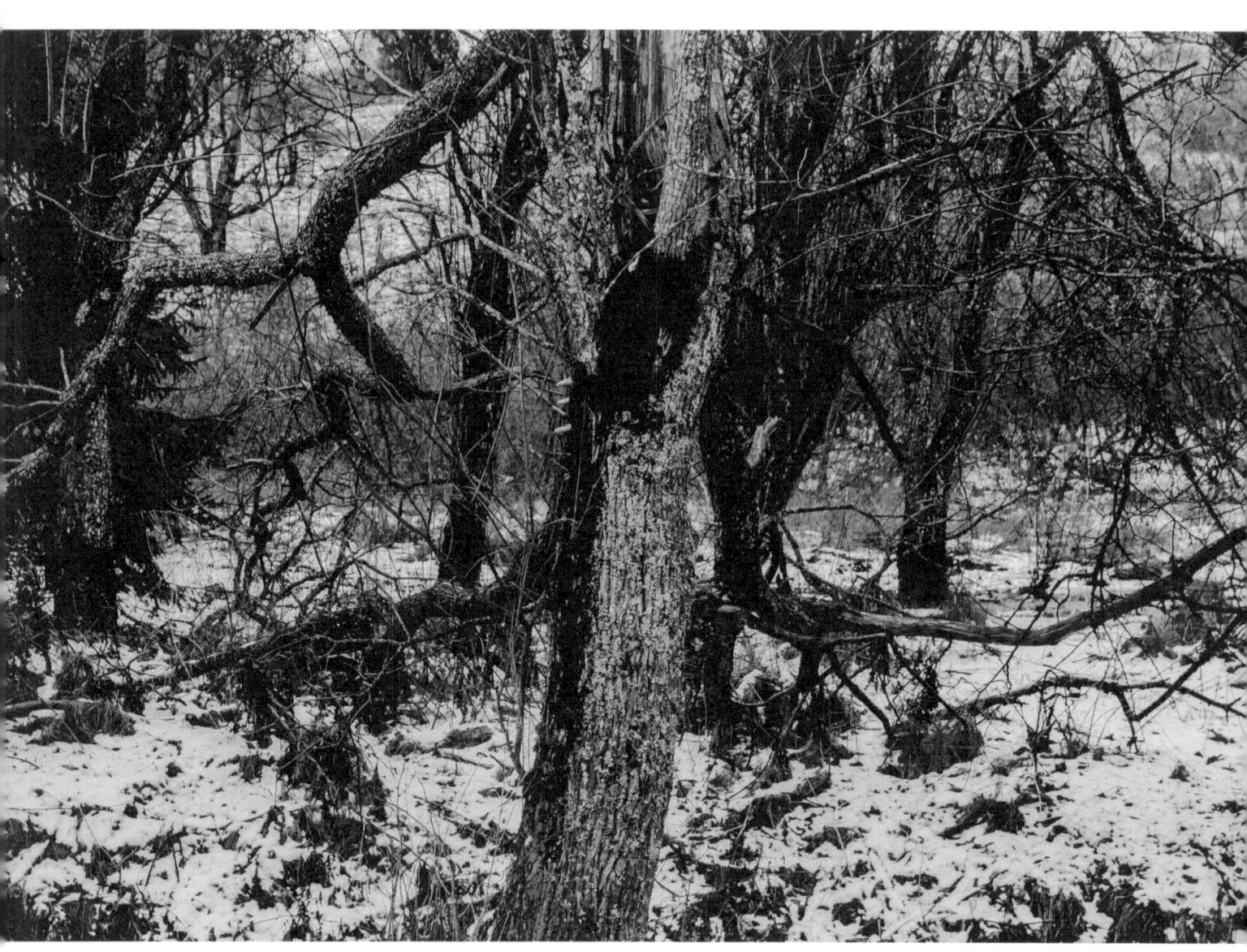

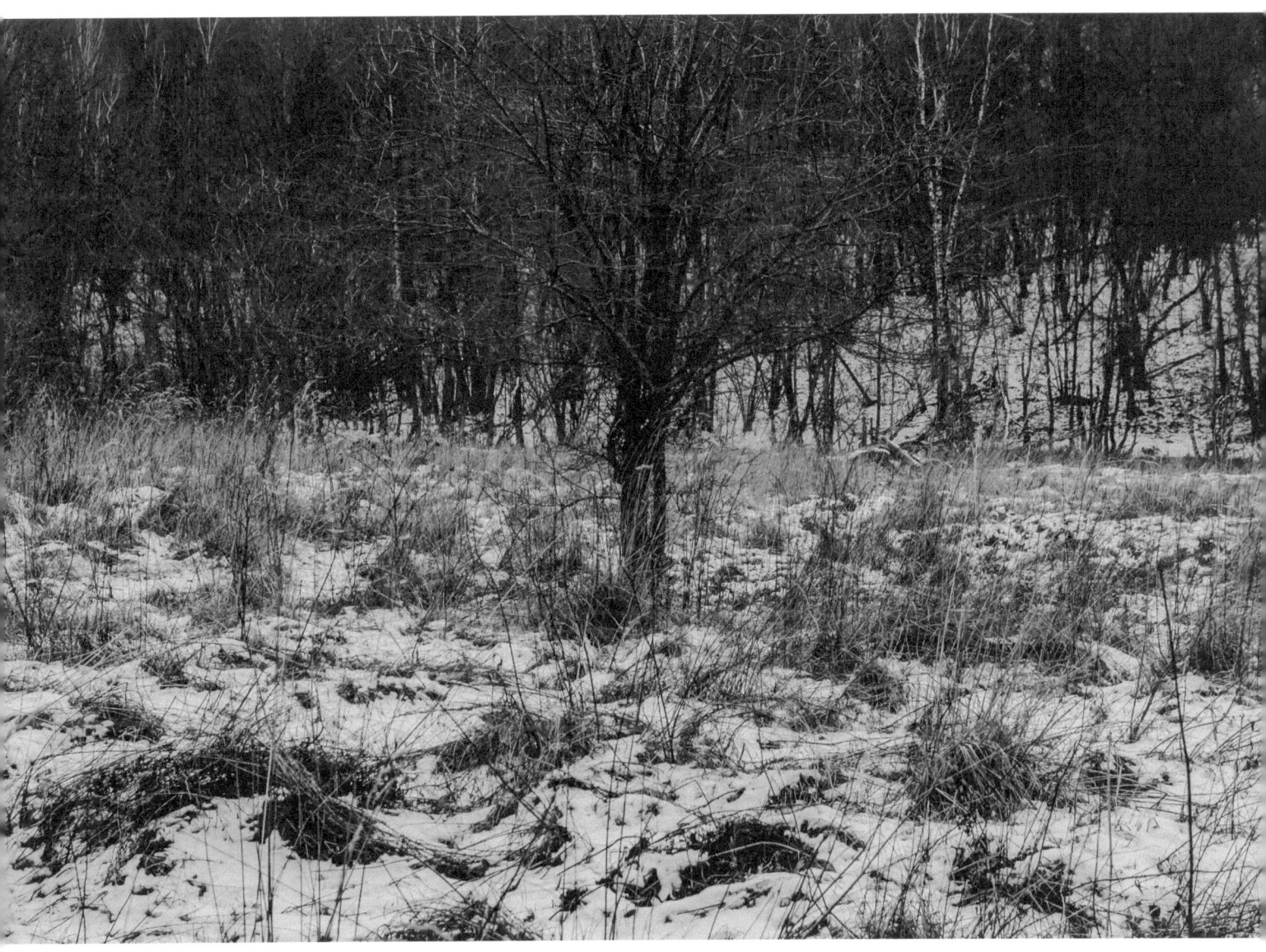

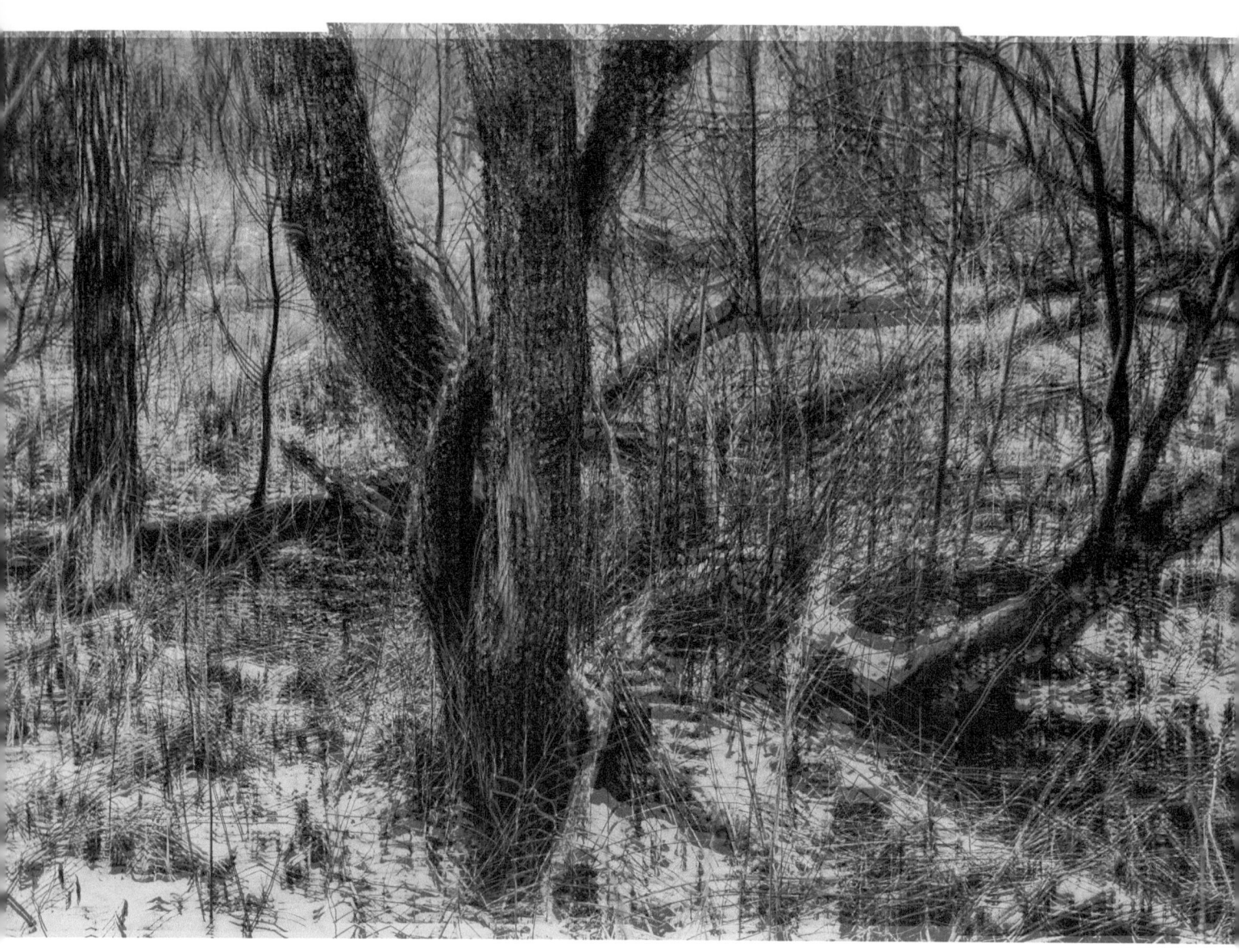

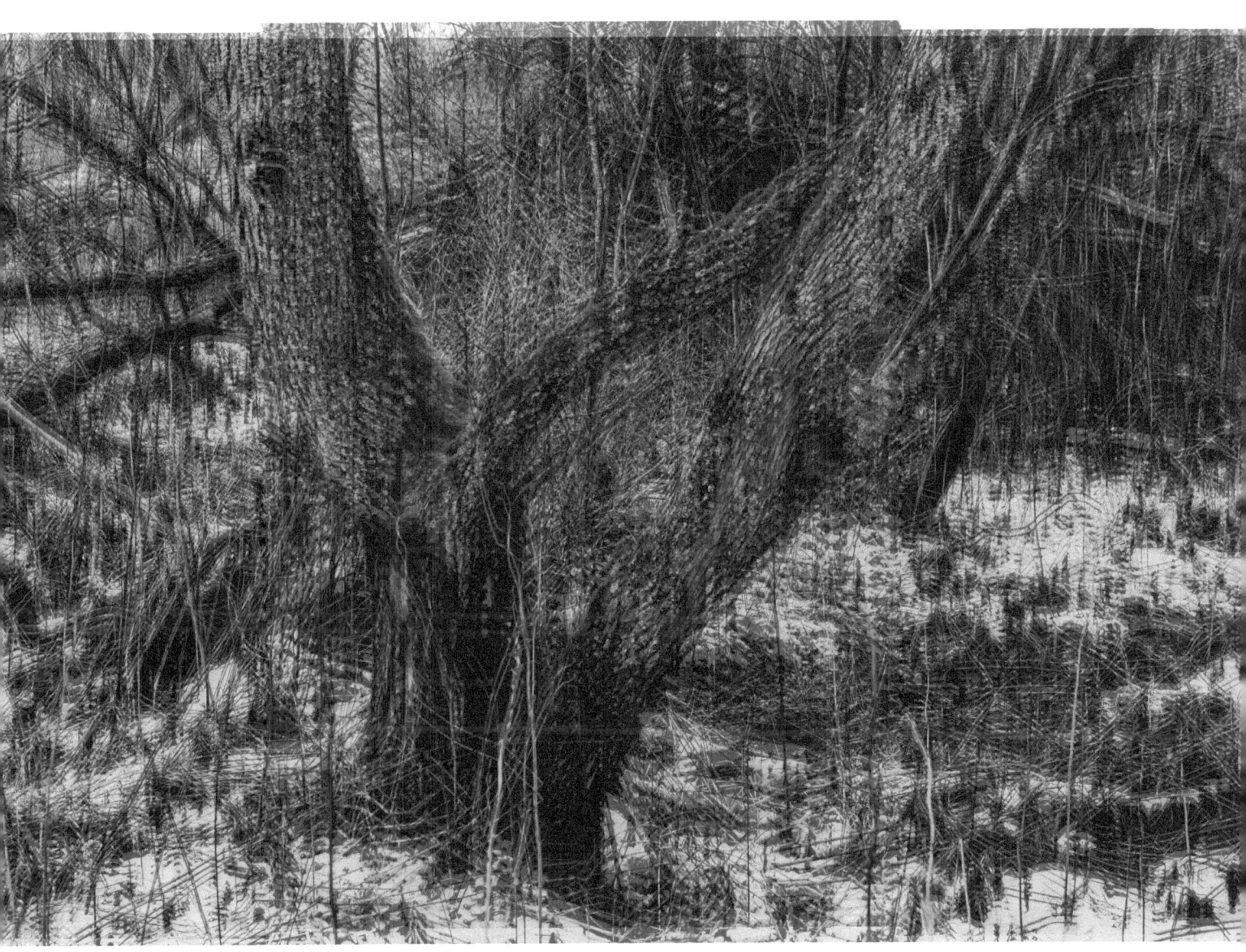

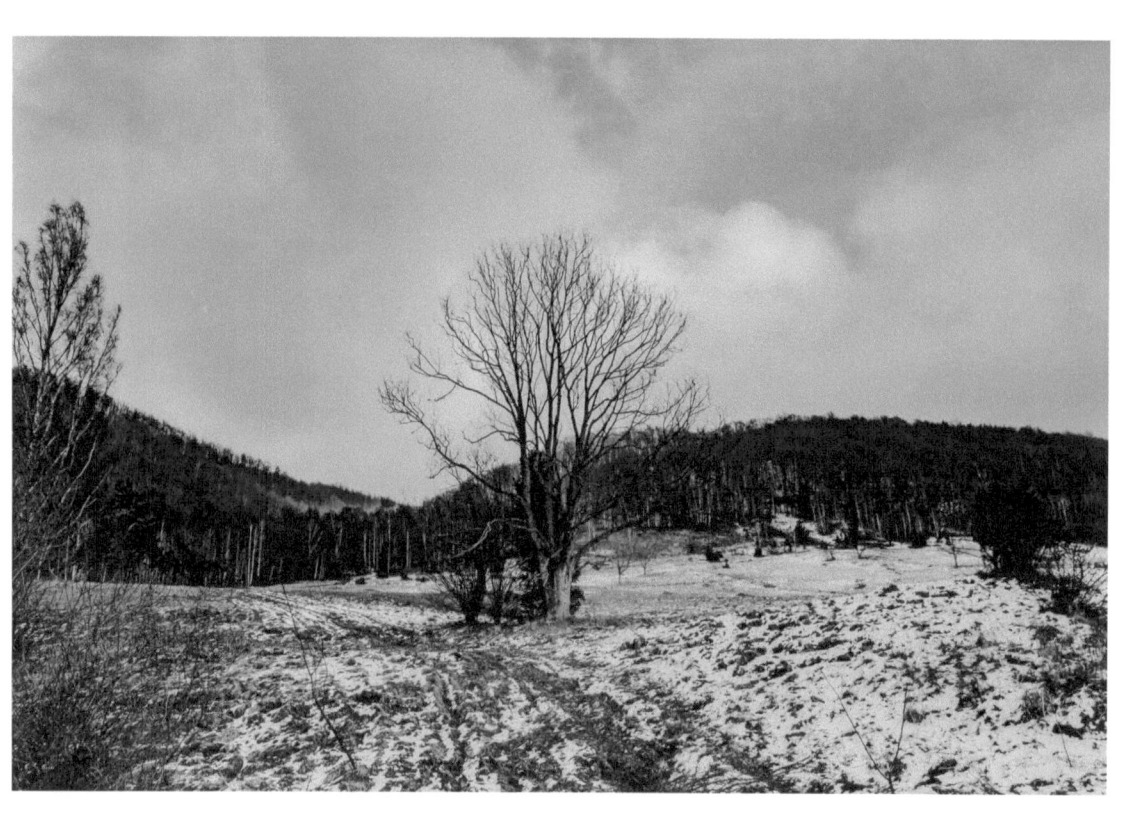

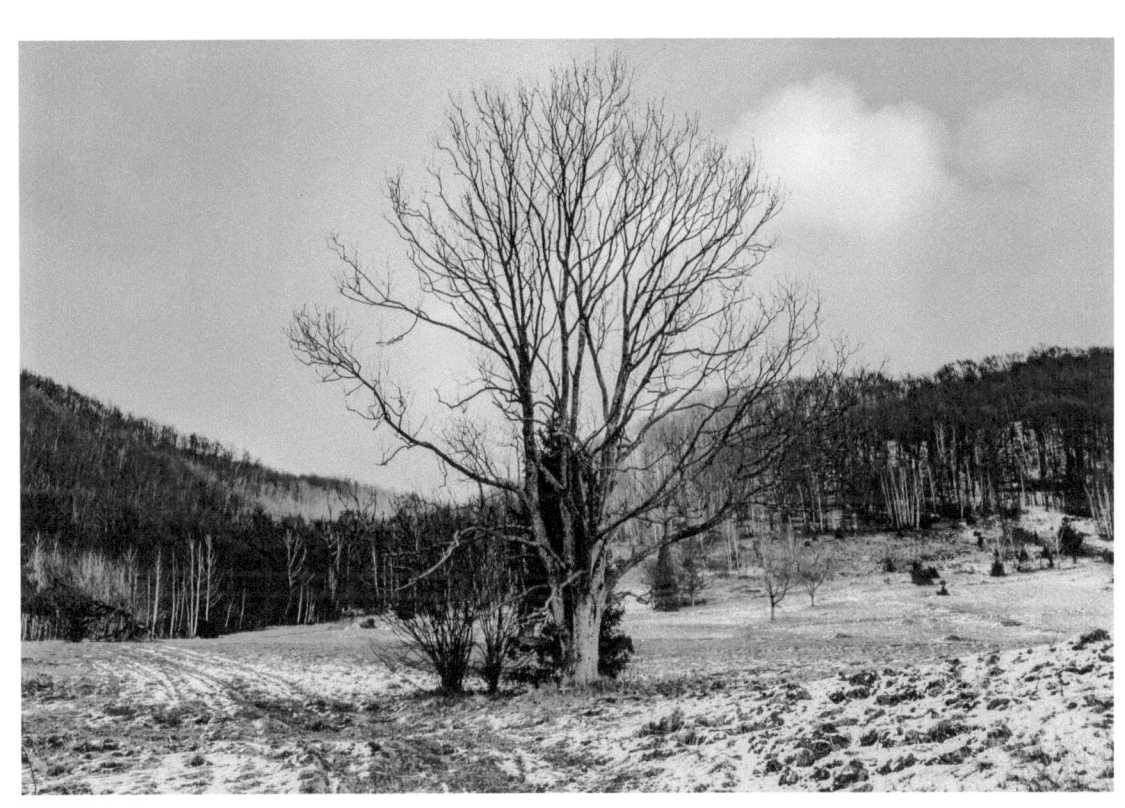

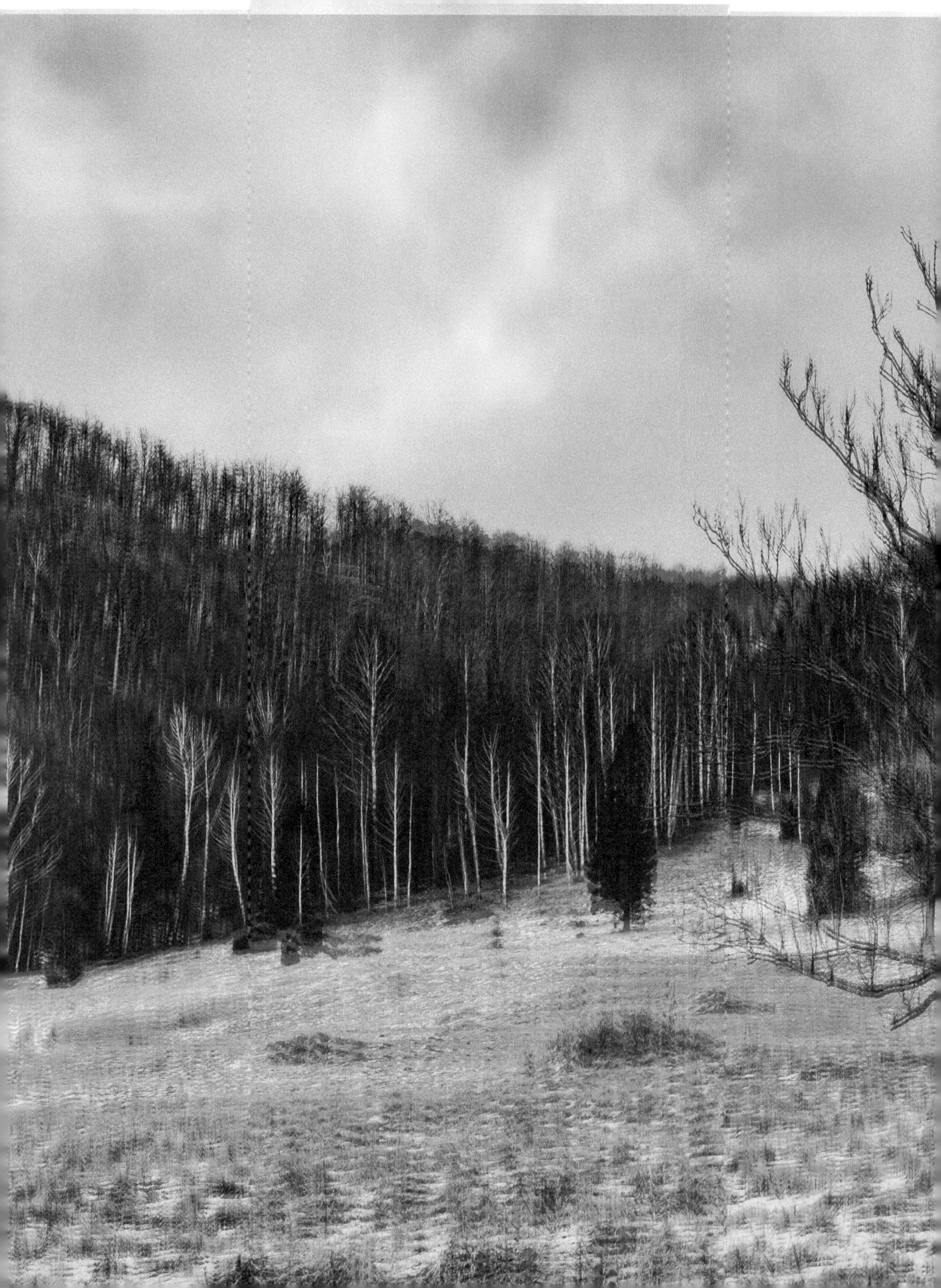

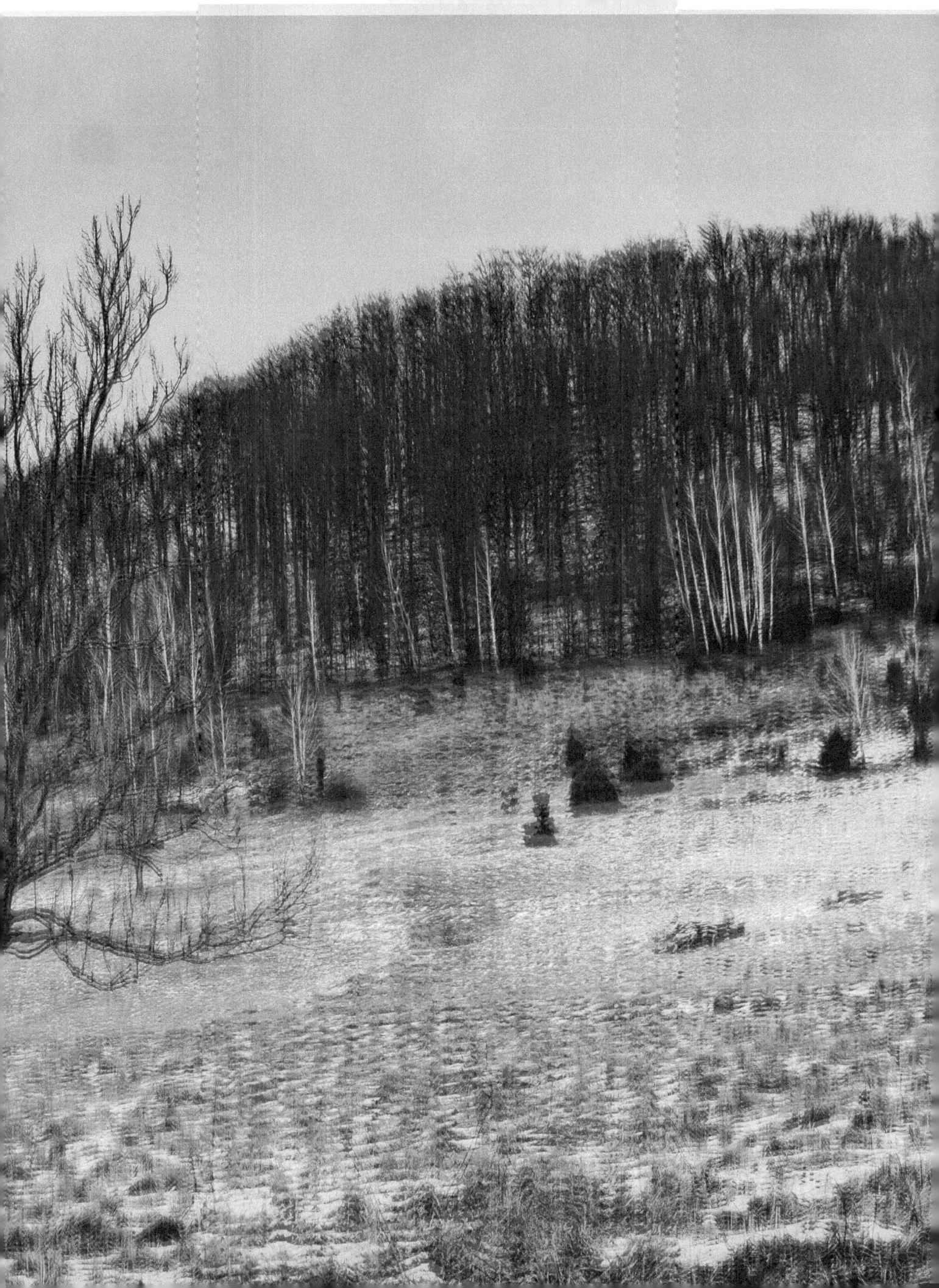

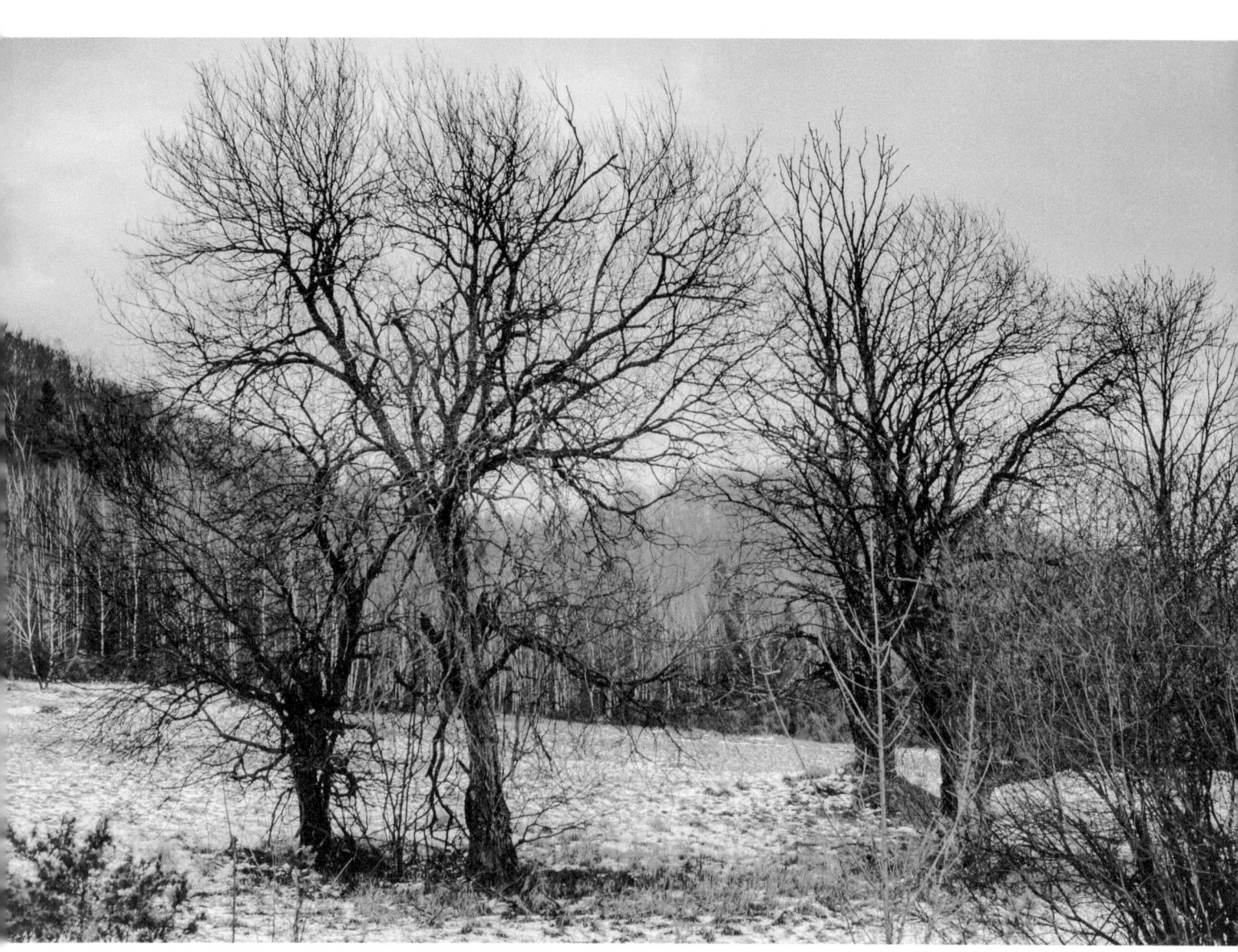

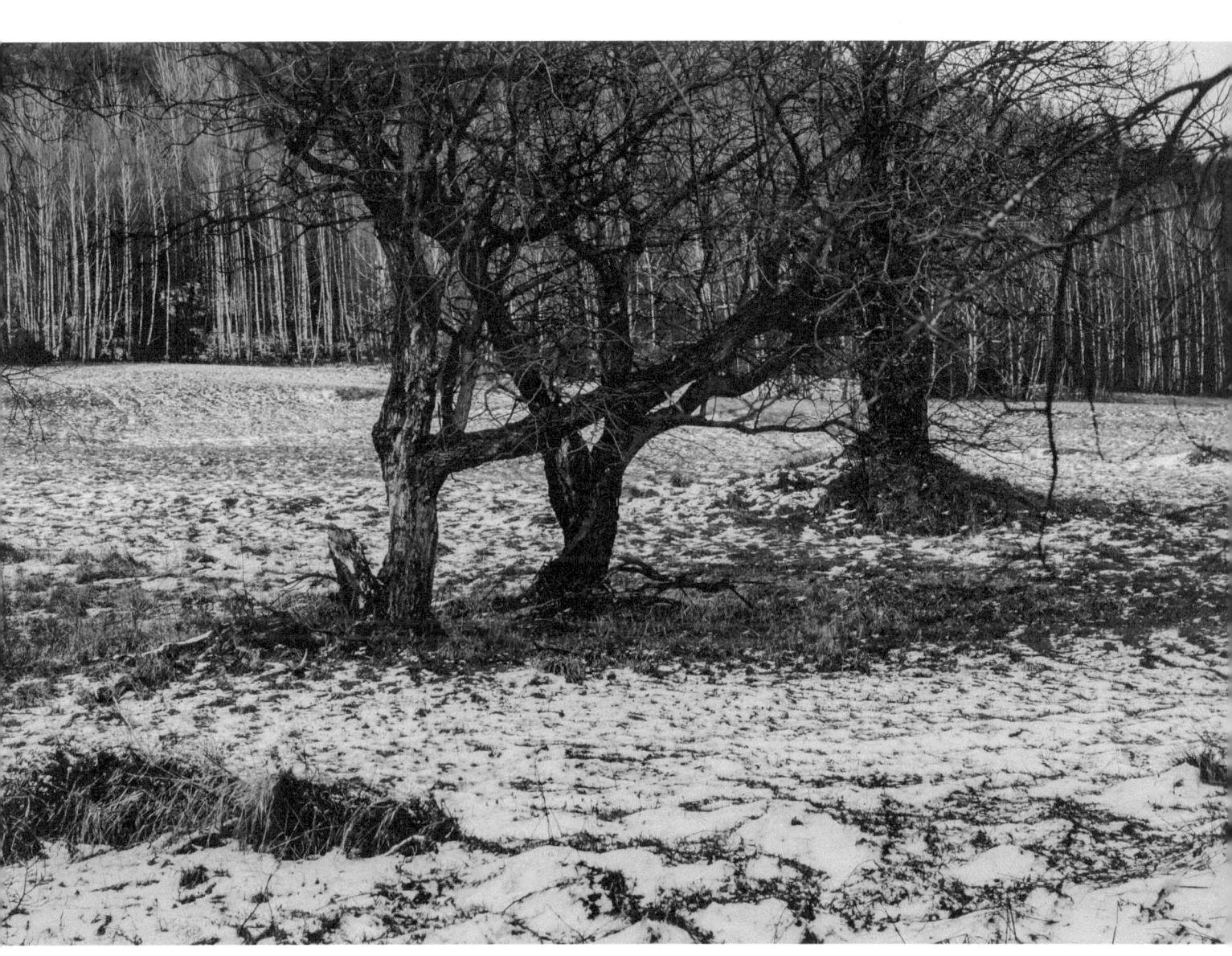

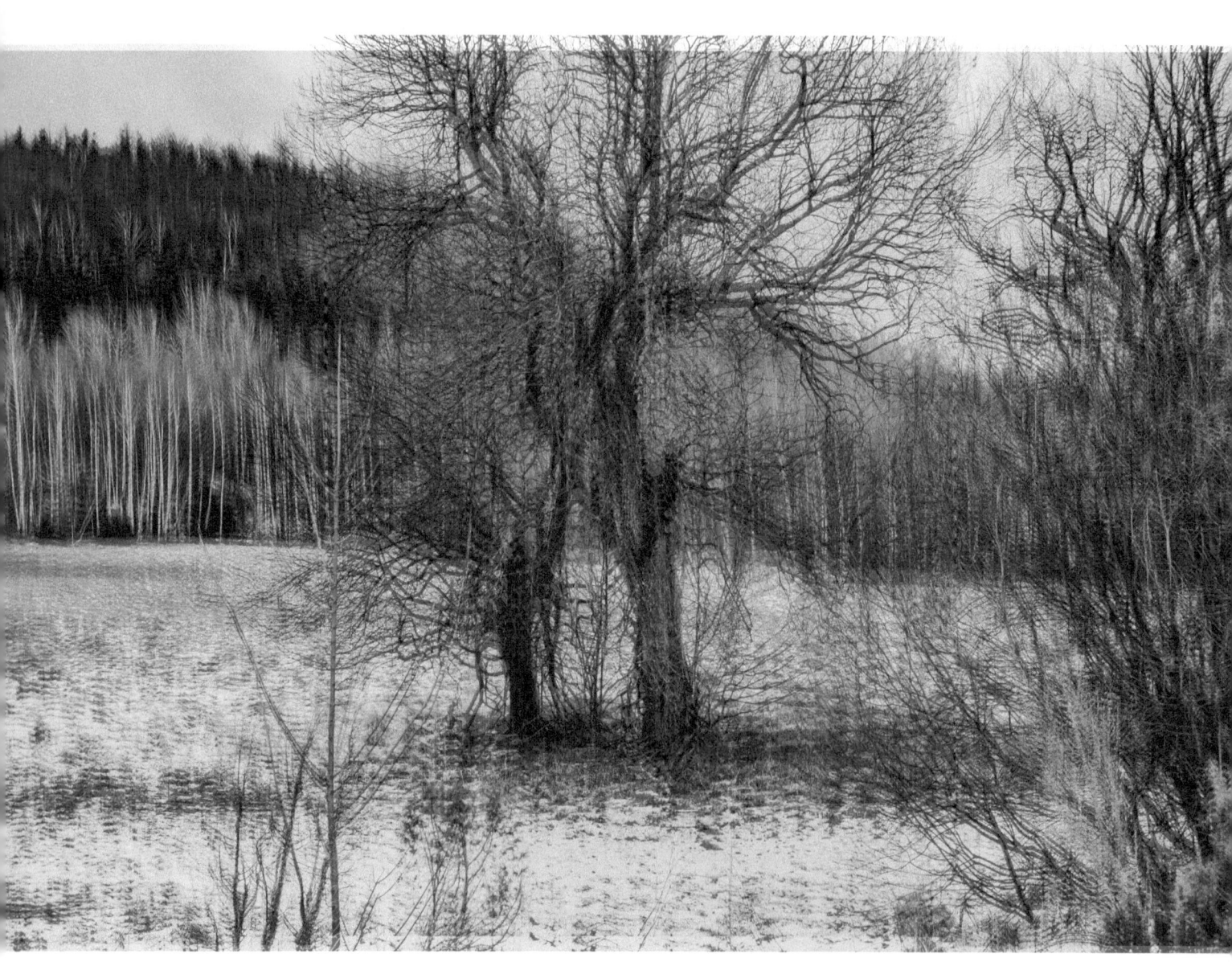

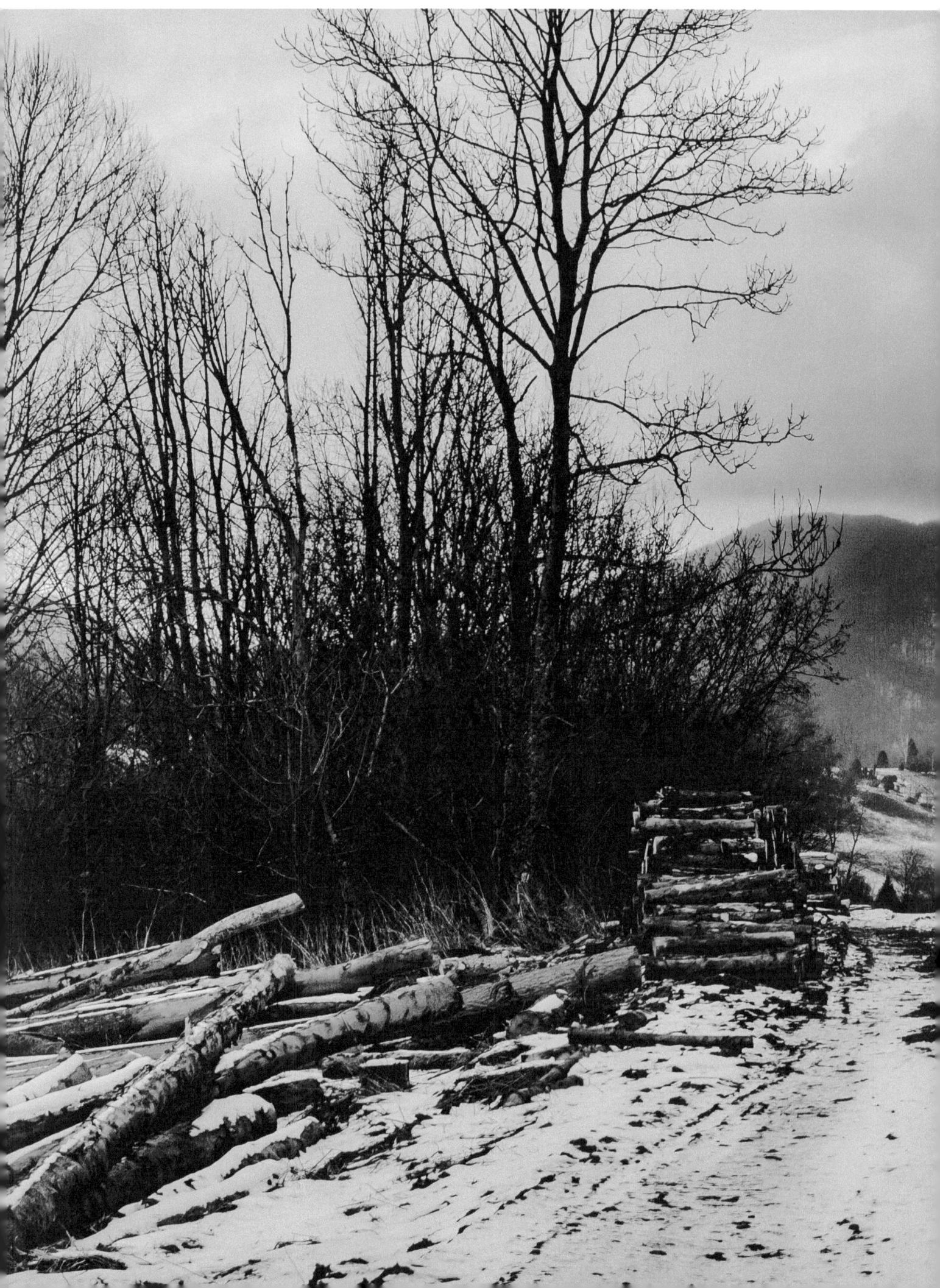

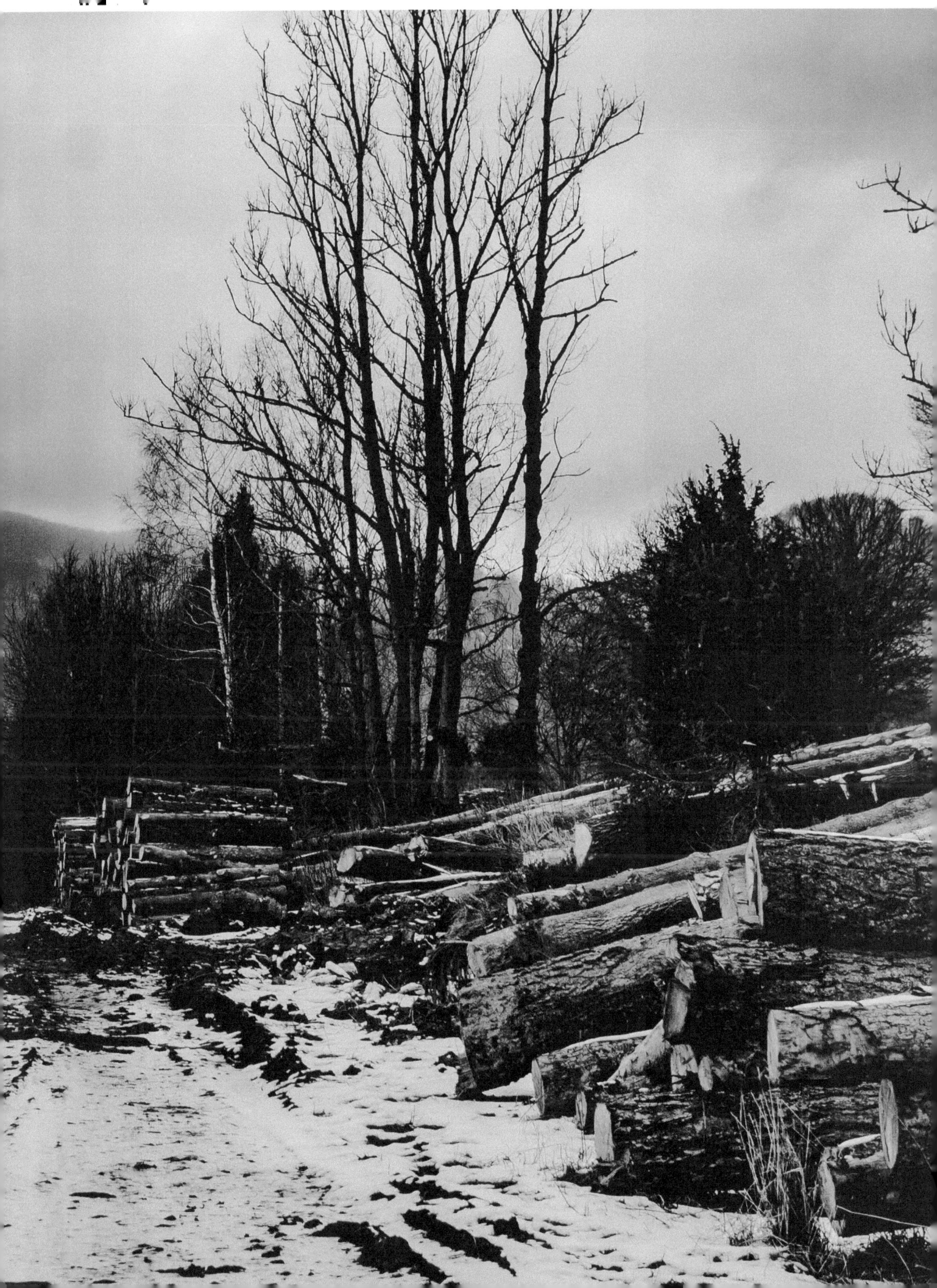

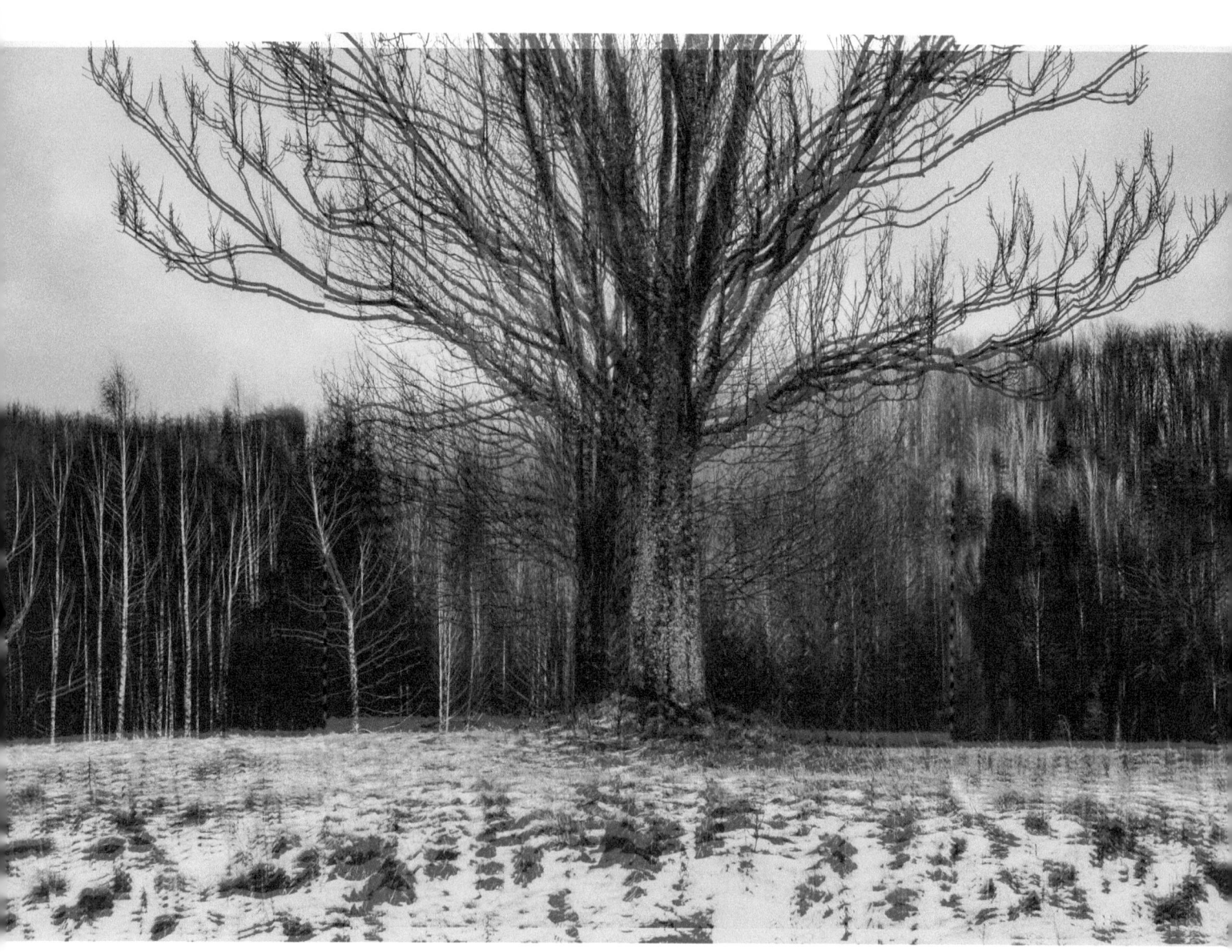

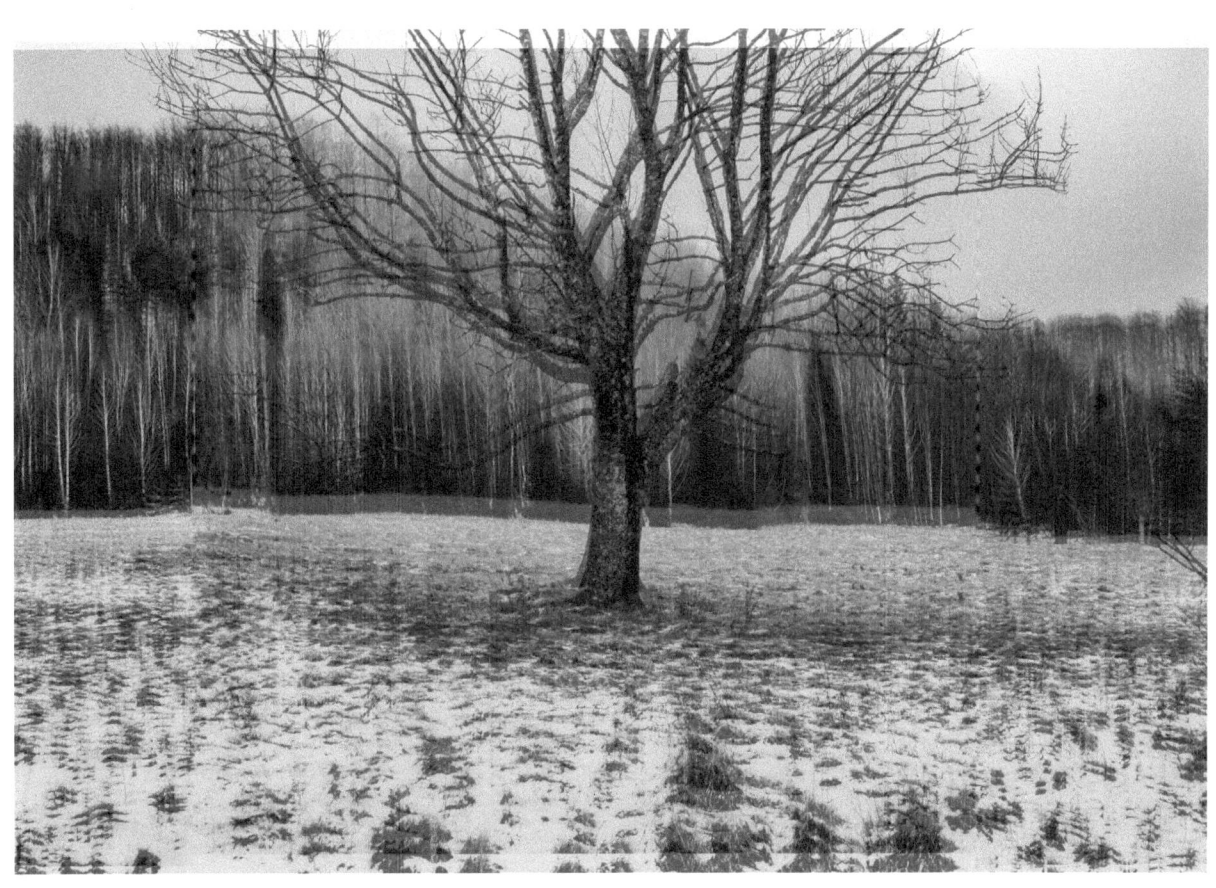

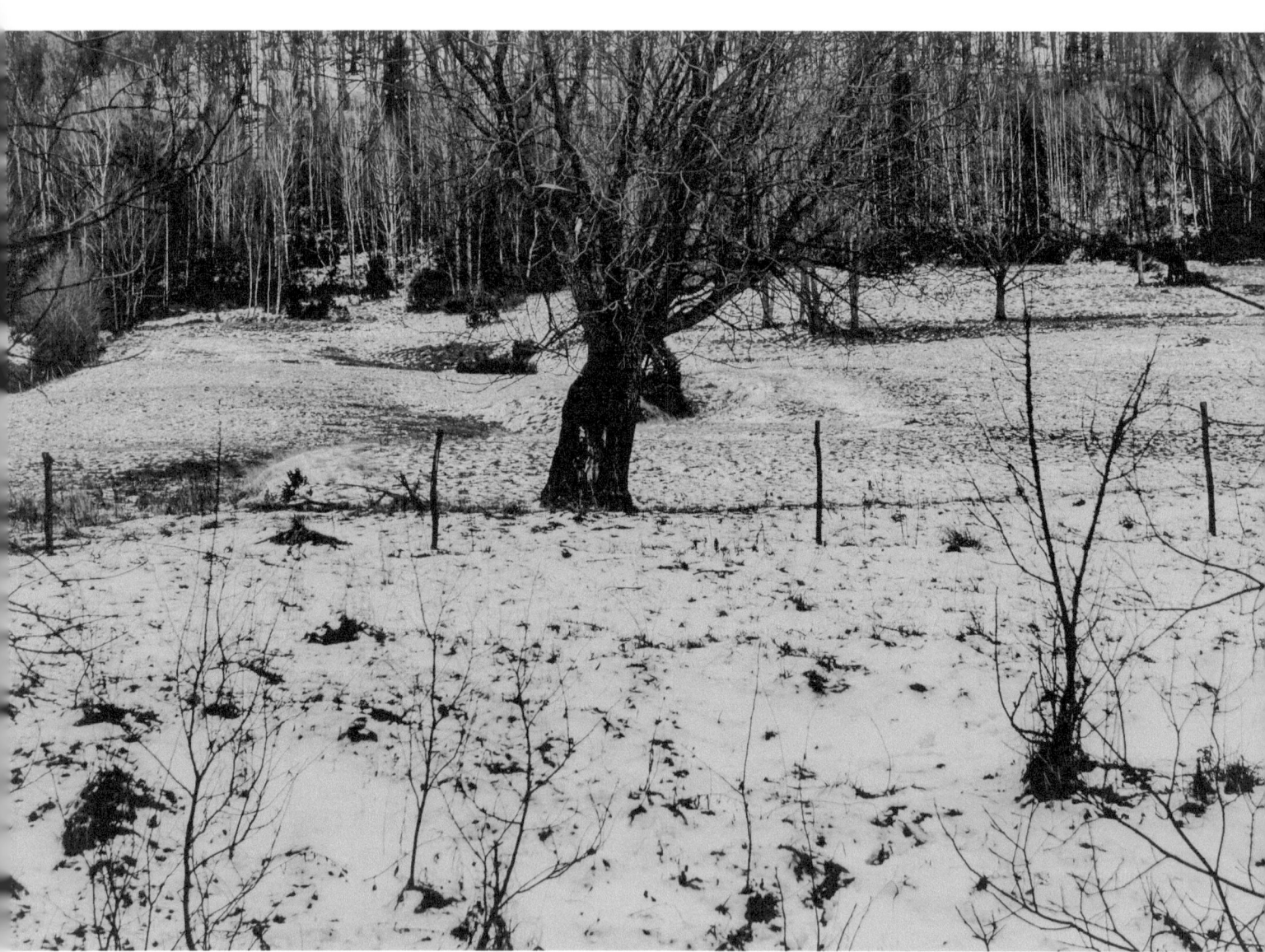

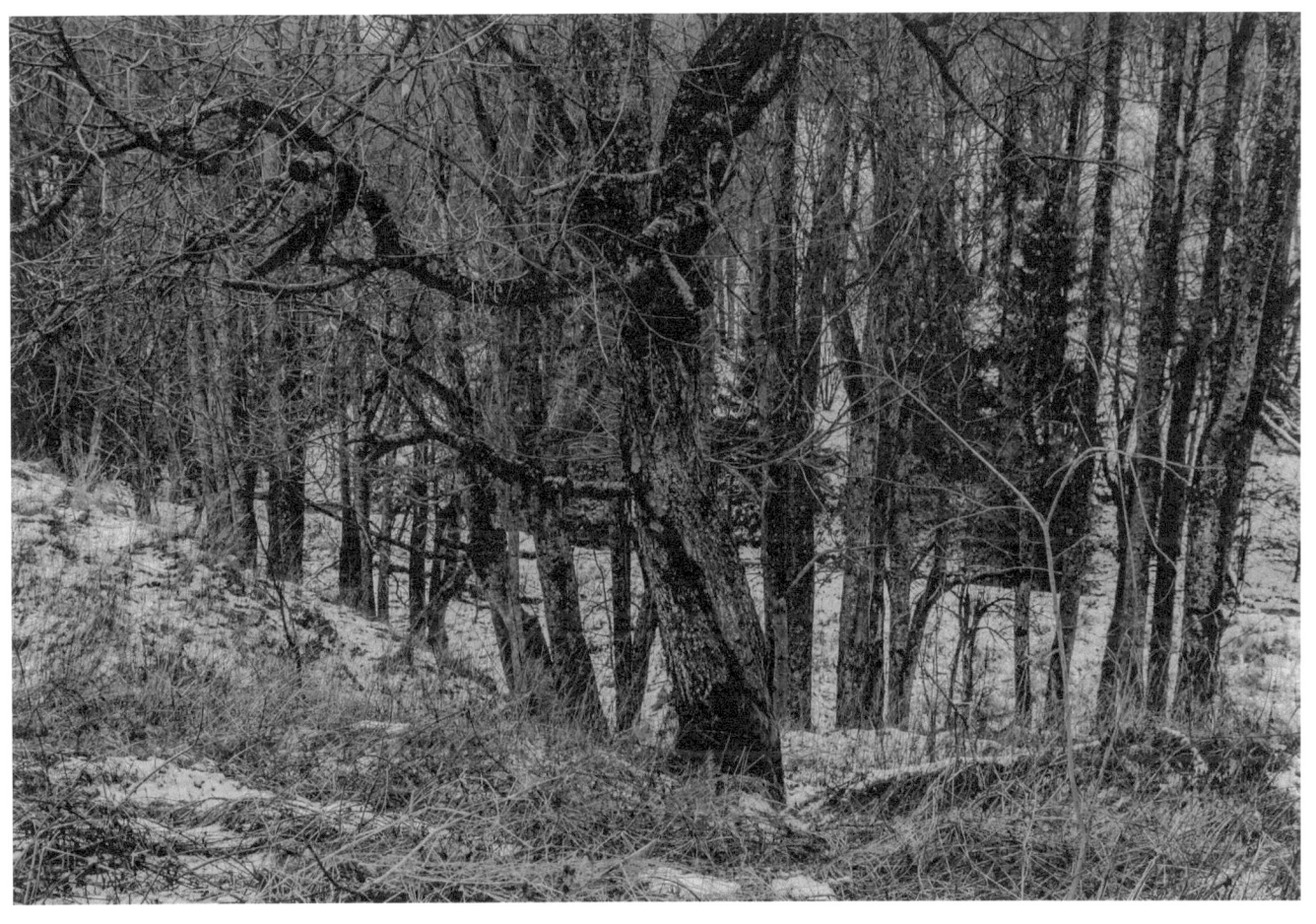

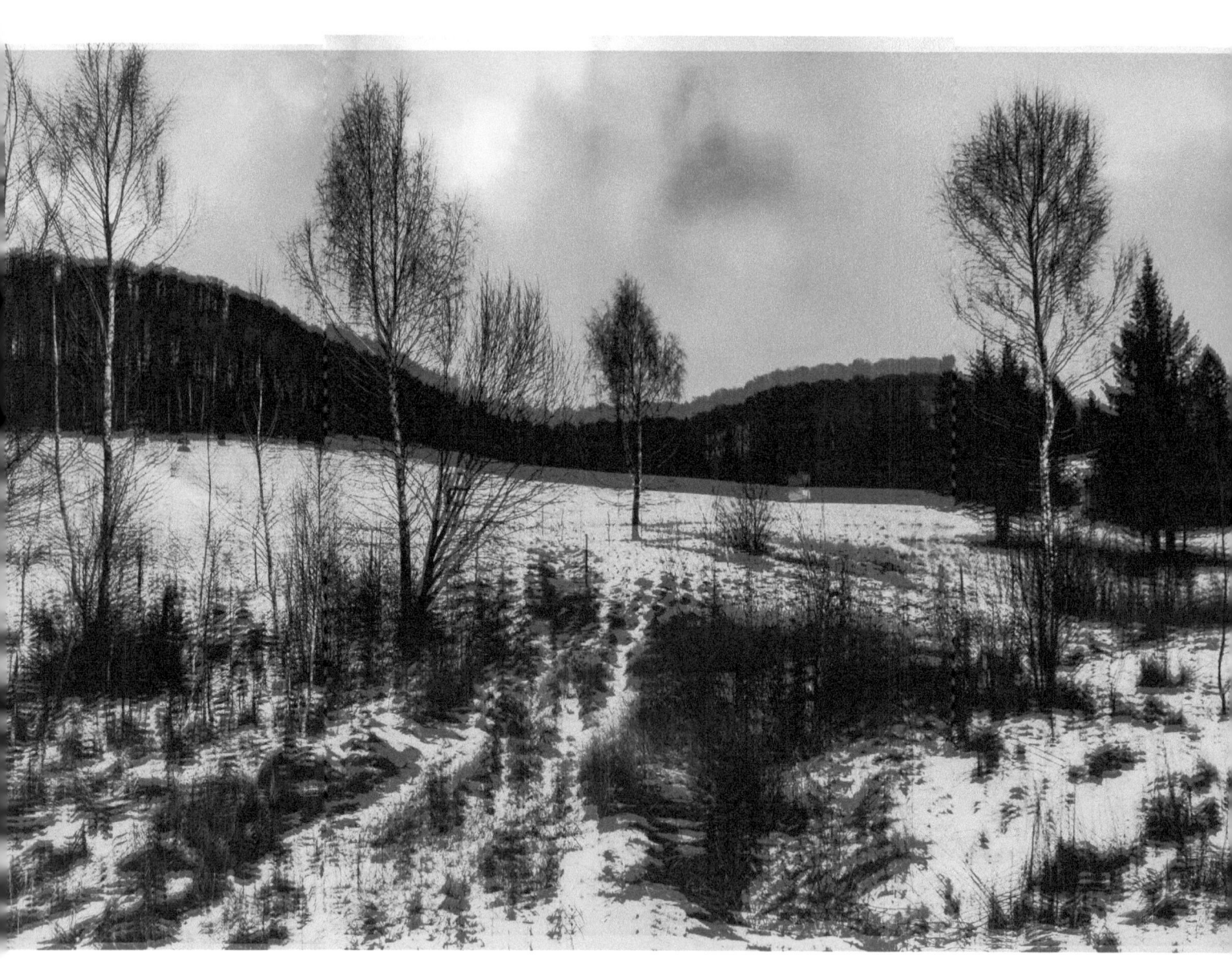

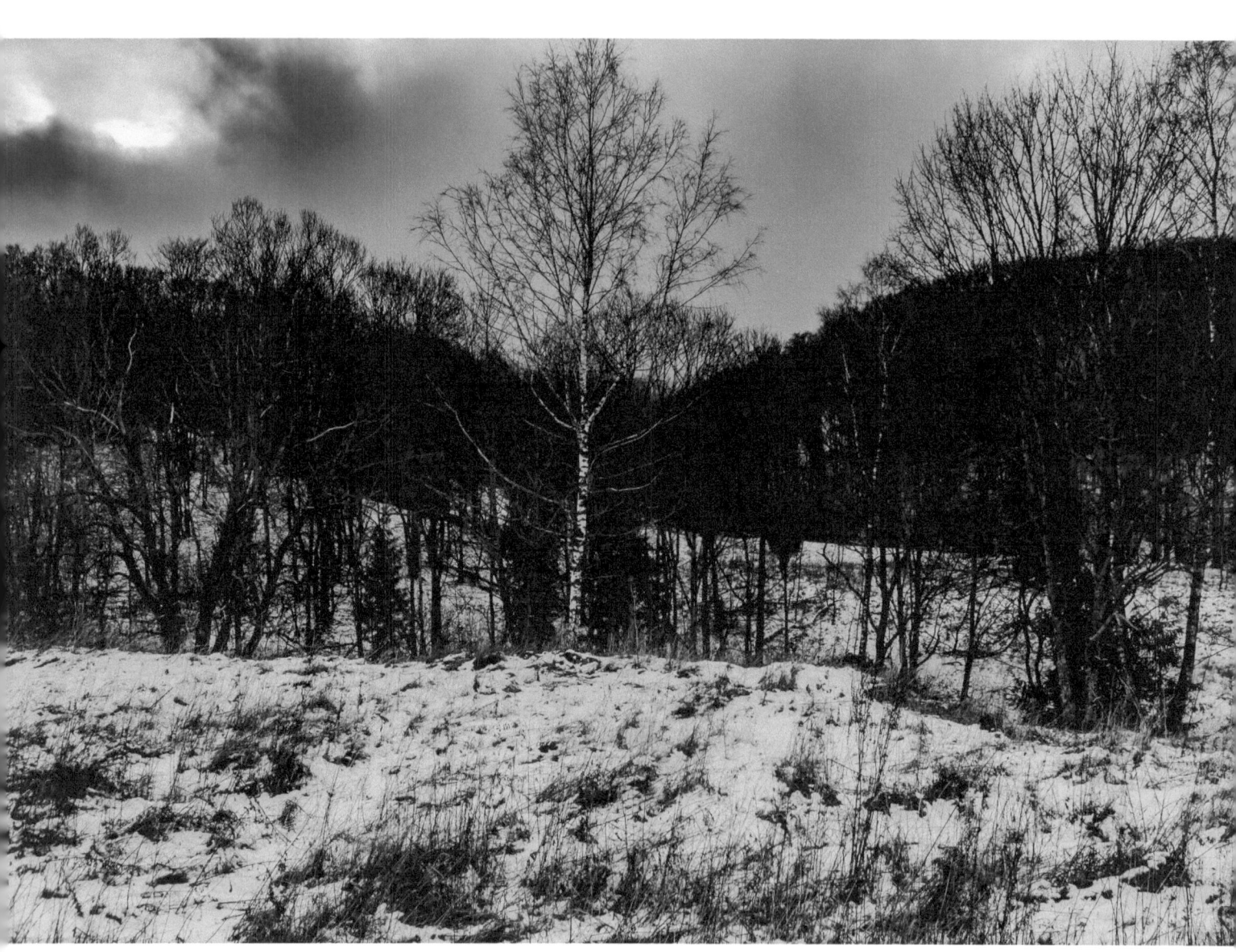

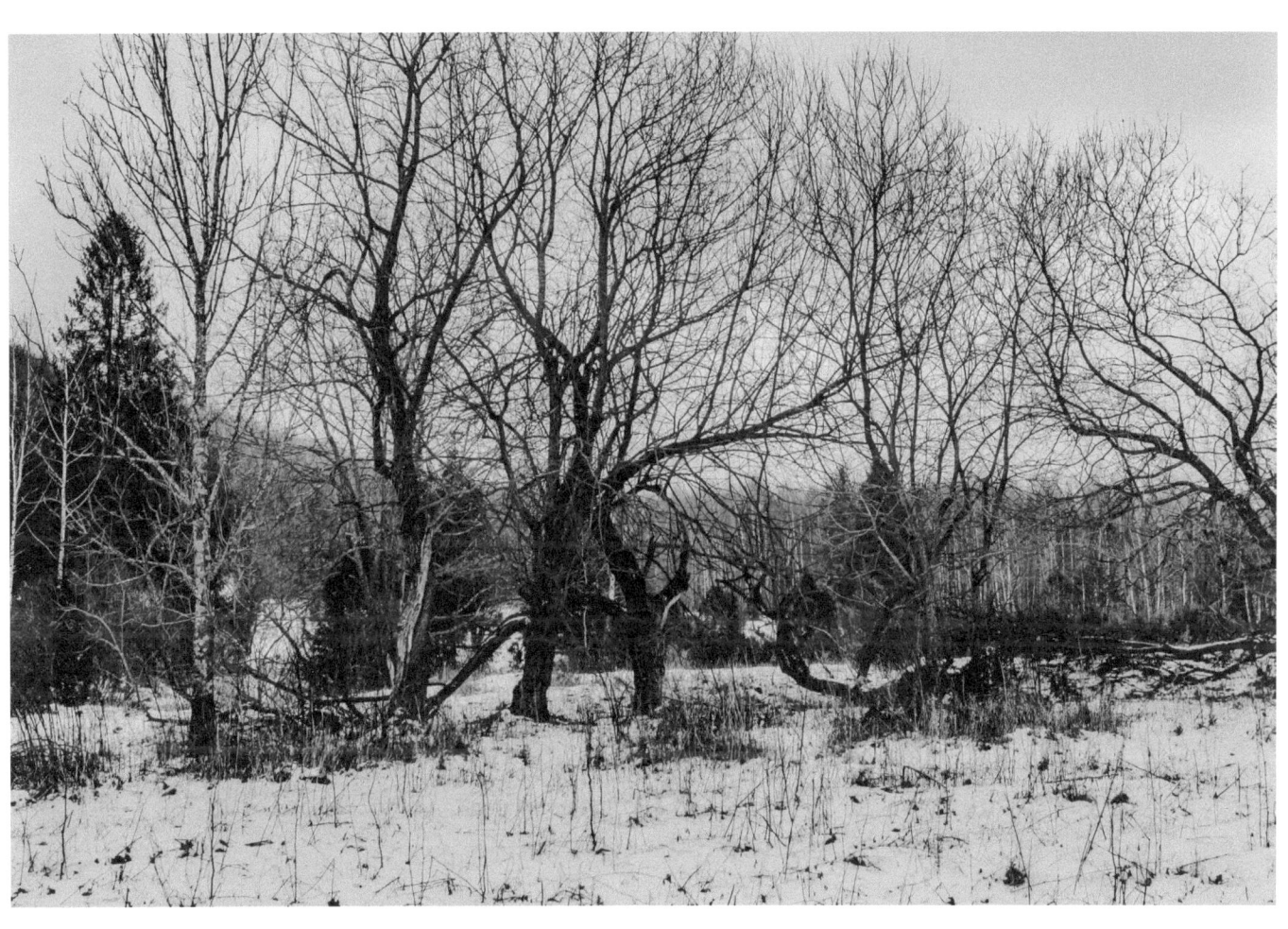

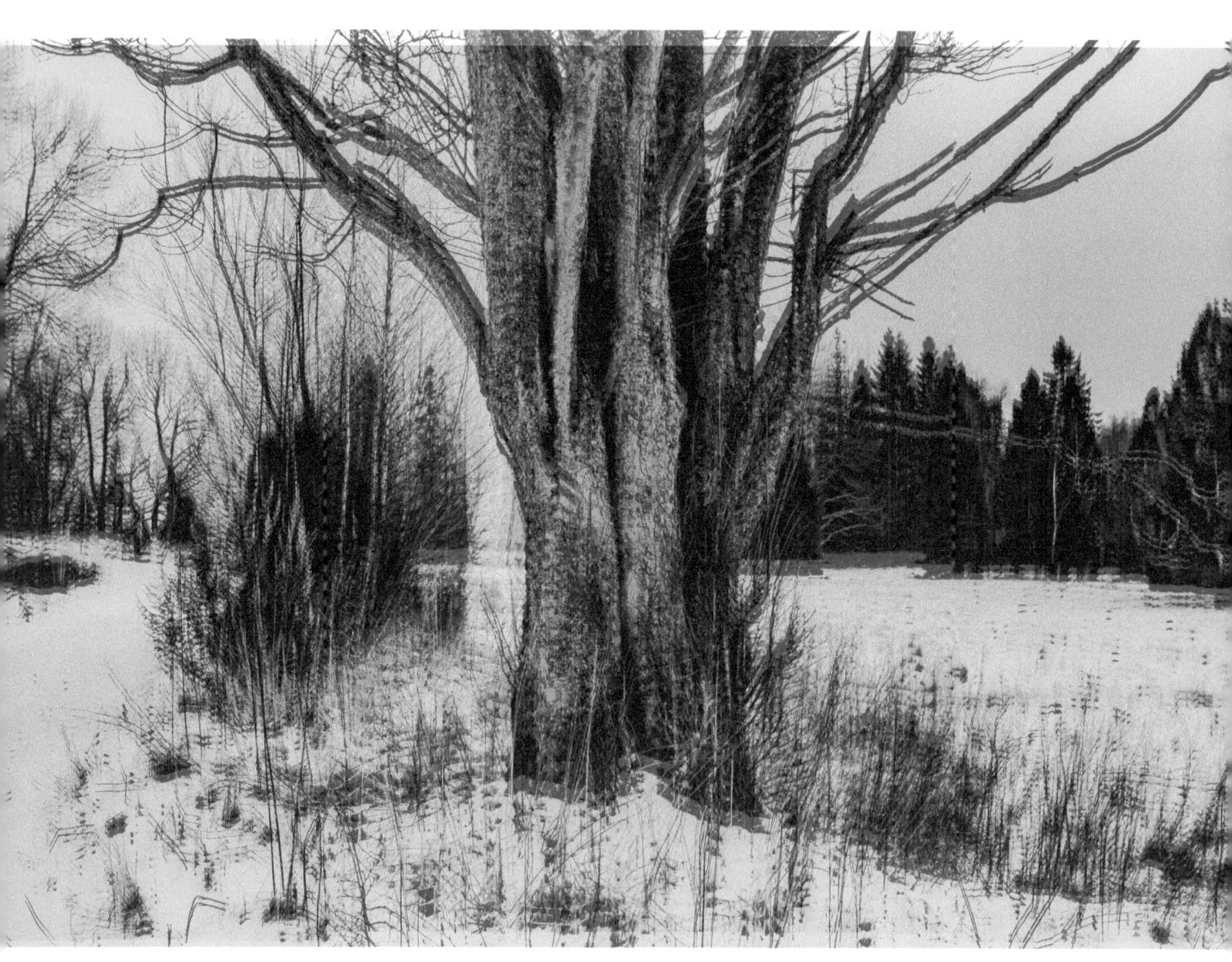

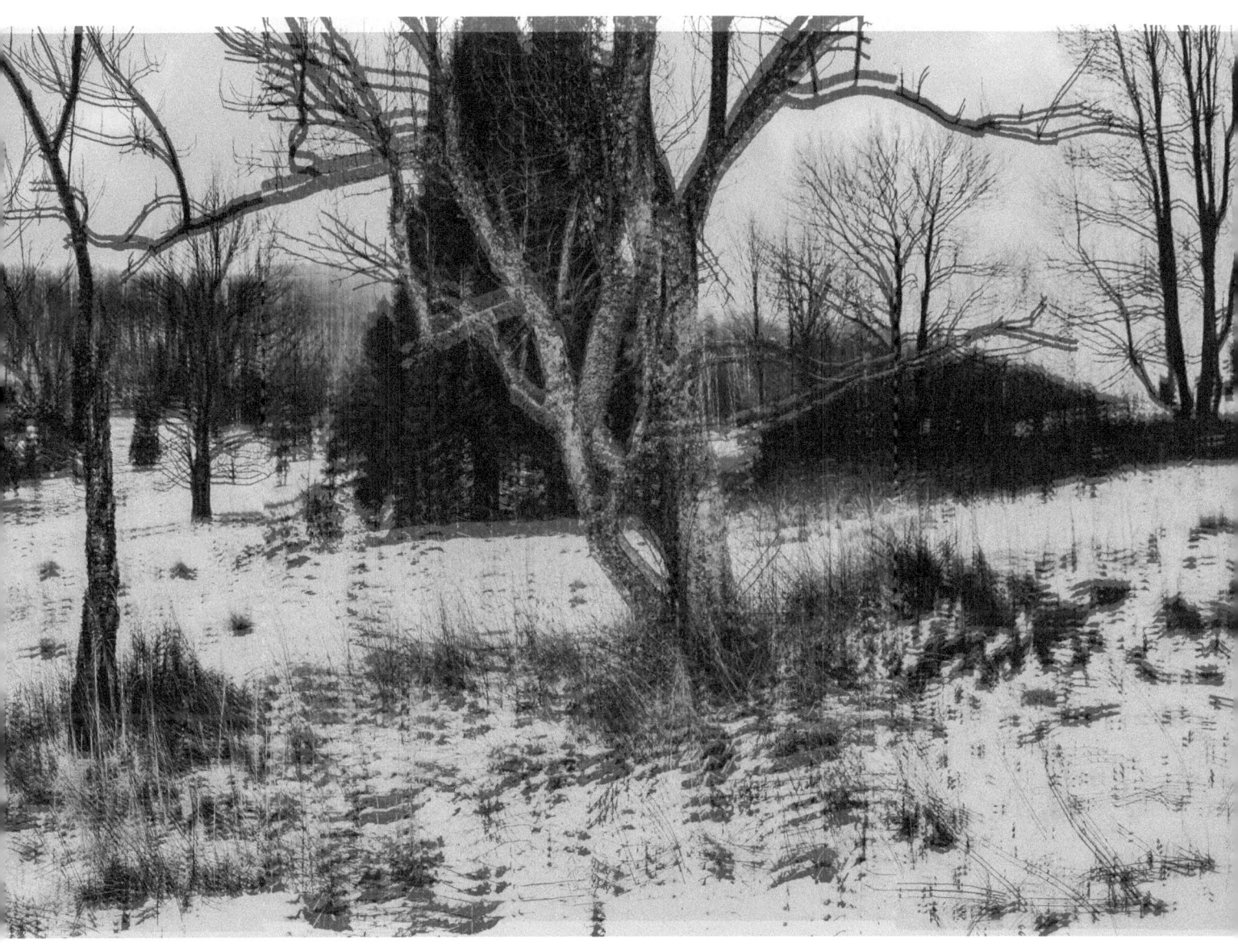

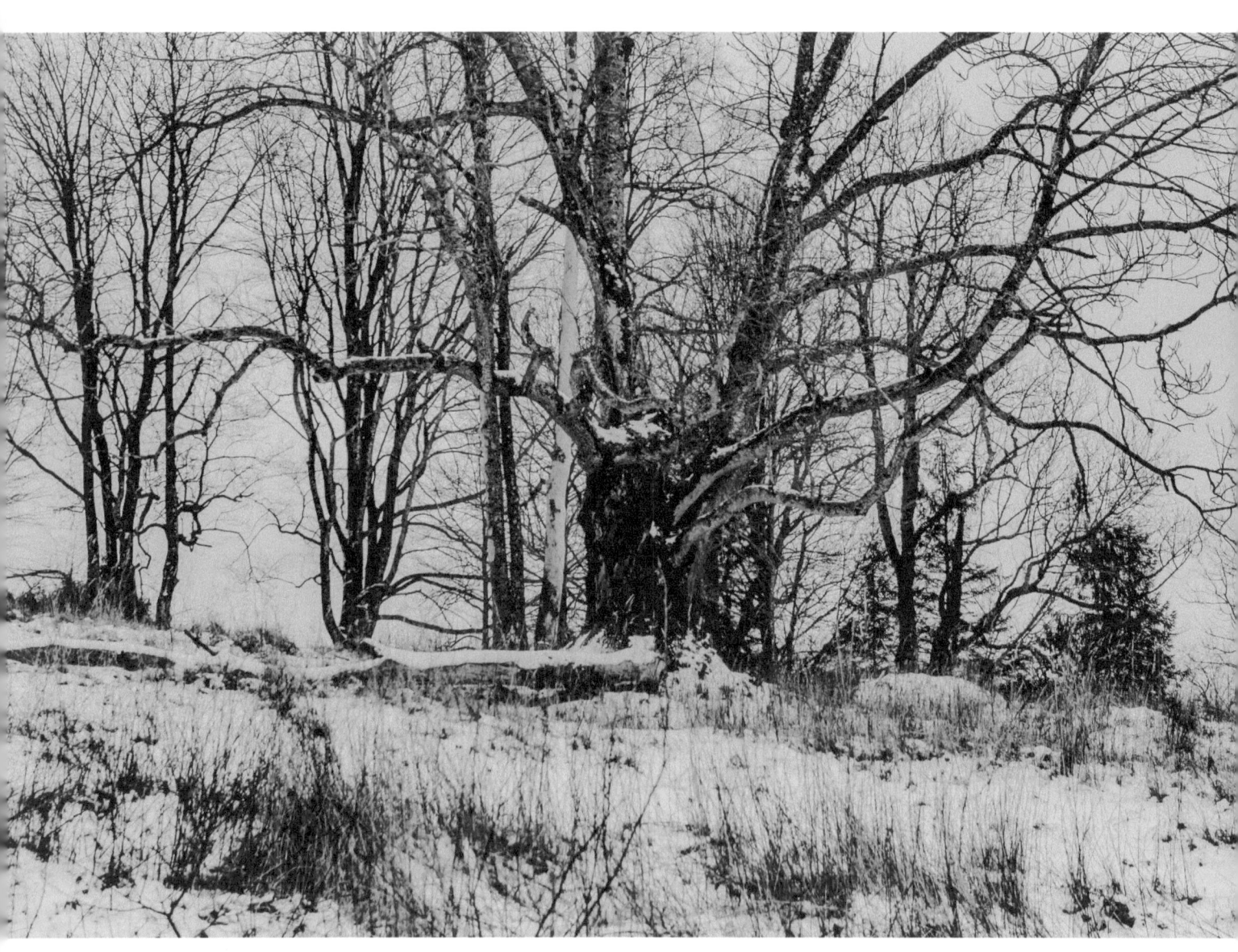

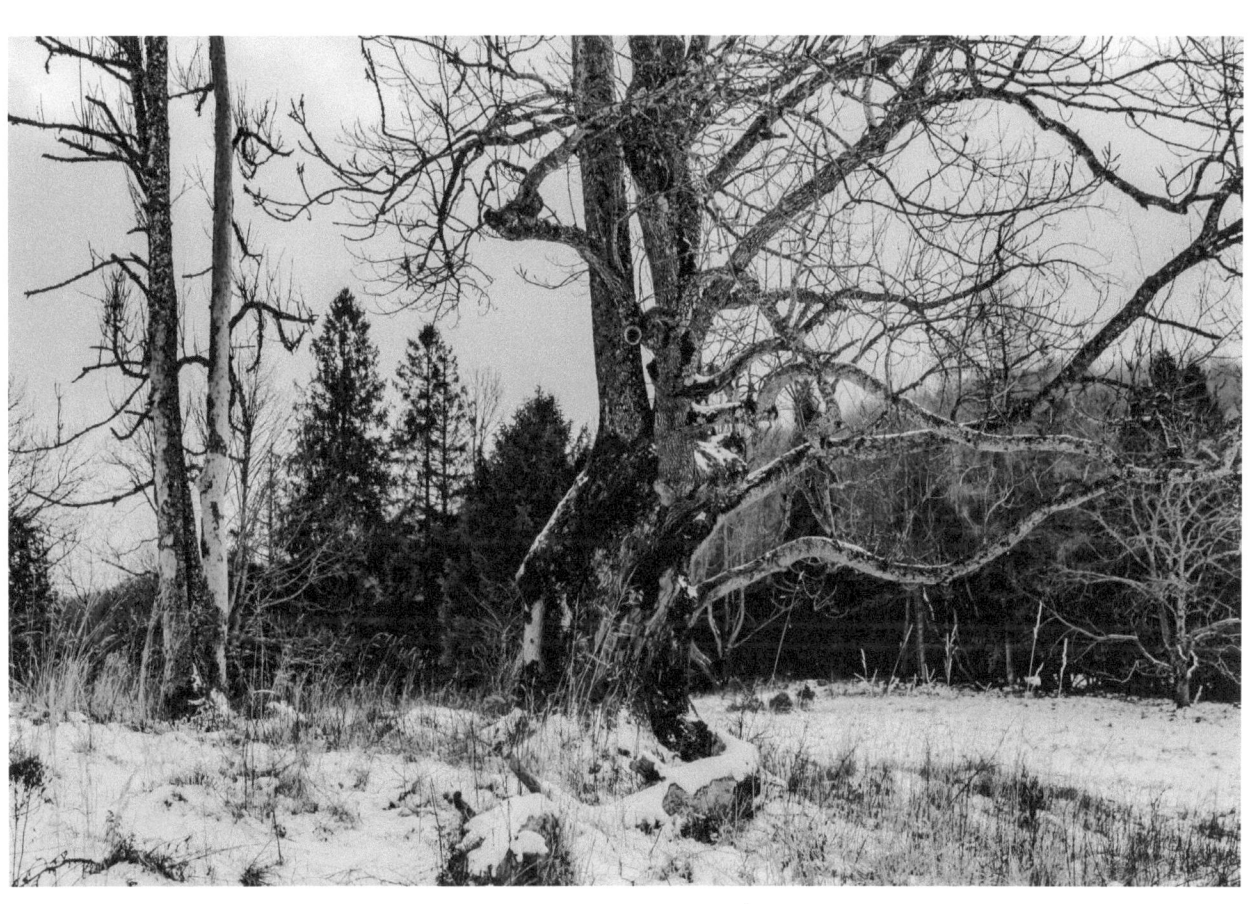

About author

I live in Poland. I photographed for many years and photography has been in the centre of my professional life since 2005. I am active at in many areas of photography: theater, fashion, street, document.
I realized several photo projects.
In 2012 and 2018 I was a stipendist of the minister of culture in Poland. My photos have featured in many publications and I have produced artwork and promotional images for artists, theatres and newspapers. I was exhibited in various exhibitions in Poland mostly in Katowice.

e-mail: jaceklidwin@wp.pl
phone: +48 663 184 900

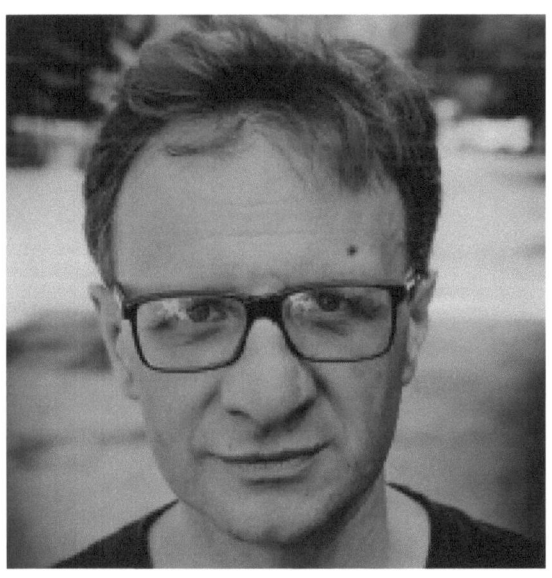

Stipends
Polish Ministry of Culture stipends:
2012 – Simply Stories – photographic project
2018 – Forgotten lives – photographic project
Marshal of The Silesian Voivodeship stipends in the field of culture:
2008 – Fragments of Ancient Names – Jewish cemeteries in Silesian Voivodeship – photographic project
2011 – A photo album about theater festivals A Part from 1998 to 2011
2014 – Ecce Homo – photographic project about homeless people
Individual exhibitions in Katowice in Poland
2003 – The Photographs That Were Taken in Szopienice – street photography
2008 – Unknown People – street photography
2009 – Human, space, light – theatrical photography at Roundabout Art Gallery
2009 – Unknown People – street photography
2010 – Packaging for the People – fashion photography
2011 – Fragments of Ancient Names – Jewish cemeteries in Silesian Voivodeship at The Archdiocesan Museum
2011/2012 – Presentation of the book about the festival A Part at Polish Radio Building

Book credits

Photos and texts: Jacek Lidwin

Cover and interior page layauts: Jacek Lidwin

Published by Jacek Lidwin

Copyright © 2020 by Jacek Lidwin

www.ingramcontent.com/pod-product-compliance
Lightning Source LLC
Chambersburg PA
CBHW051925210526
45473CB00006B/2140